Environment
and
Behavior
A Dynamic Perspective

THE PLENUM SOCIAL ECOLOGY SERIES

Series Editor: Rudolf Moos
*Stanford University, Stanford, California and
Veterans Administration Hospital, Palo Alto, California*

Environment and Utopia ● Rudolf Moos and Robert Brownstein

Environment and Behavior: *A Dynamic Perspective* ● Charles J. Holahan

Environment and Behavior
A Dynamic Perspective

Charles J. Holahan
The University of Texas at Austin

PLENUM PRESS . NEW YORK AND LONDON

Library of Congress Cataloging in Publication Data

Holahan, Charles J
 Environment and behavior.

 (The Plenum social ecology series)
 Includes bibliographies and index.
 1. Environmental psychology. 2. Architecture—Psychological aspects. I. Title.
 BF353.H65   155.9   77-25400
 ISBN 0-306-31086-4

© 1978 Plenum Press, New York
A Division of Plenum Publishing Corporation
227 West 17th Street, New York, N.Y. 10011

Printed in the United States of America

To
my mother and father
and
Carole

Preface

This book has been written as a text for advanced undergraduate students and graduate students in the burgeoning field of study that has come to be called *environment and behavior*. It is appropriate for courses in environmental psychology, social ecology, ecological psychology, and community psychology when the community is conceptualized from an ecological viewpoint. In addition, the book may be used in design courses oriented toward an appreciation of the interaction between architecture and human behavior.

The book presents a thorough explication of a perspective or viewpoint in approaching the study of environment and behavior, which has tended to be underemphasized in past work in this area. The dynamic perspective focuses on the active role people play in dealing with environmental challenges. Its investigative interest is in the processes that mediate the effects of environment on behavior, especially the positive and adaptive ways in which people cope with the environment. The accent is on the creative, complex, yet subtle character of these environmental processes.

The recent history of environmental psychology has been characterized by two chief types of scholarly endeavor — an attempt to initiate theoretical development and an effort to accumulate an extensive data base for the field. I believe both of these activities can profit by an explicit consideration of the guiding perspectives that underlie conceptual advance and research investigation. For, although a perspective is itself pretheoretical, its underlying influence shapes to a considerable degree both the type of data we are likely to collect and the kinds of theory we are inclined to evolve. In order to enhance the relevance of the perspective discussed here to research inquiry in environmental psychology, a particular effort has been made in preparing this book to include a wide diversity of types of environmental research studies, which I have conducted over a seven-year period, in support of the dynamic perspective. The research projects selected for the book are especially broad-based in terms of the environmental settings investigated, the human processes studied, and the research designs and types of measures employed.

It is hoped that students will be particularly attracted to the book's emphasis on people and the exciting and interesting ways in which people behave in dealing with their environment. This is especially so since we have often tended in the past, as a function of the way in which we have approached environmental research, to imply an overly static, passive, and simplistic picture of environment–behavior relationships. The dynamic perspective, in contrast, offers an inherently interesting and potentially revitalizing view of the interrelationship between people and the physical settings in which they reside.

The major part of the book is composed of three sections, each of which examines a different environmental process that reflects such a dynamic perspective. Part I examines the process of *environmental coping*, showing the positive, adaptive ways in which people deal with environmental challenges in a public housing project, a university megadorm, and a psychiatric ward. Part II then views the process of *social accommodation*, detailing the subtle and active behaviors that people engage in even when negative environmental impacts cannot be avoided. Research examples are presented from an experimental hospital dayroom, a university counseling setting, and the urban environment. Next, Part III discusses the process of *environmental schematization* through which individuals impose personal meaning on their definition of the physical environment. Examples are offered from research involving sex differences in environmental perception and errors in cognitive mapping.

In addition, an initial and a closing chapter offer a unifying framework to facilitate the student's integrating the work in terms of the dynamic perspective. Chapter 1 presents a discussion of the emergence of the dynamic perspective during seven years of research in environmental psychology. Included is a consideration of major issues in the field of environmental psychology, which offer a conceptual backdrop for the present work. Also included is a discussion of how the dynamic perspective differs from the generally established perspectives in environmental psychology. The final chapter of the book presents an integrated picture of the dynamic perspective, focusing particularly on its implications for the future development of the field of environment and behavior in the spheres of theoretical development, research methodology, and the application of scientific knowledge.

There are many individuals who warrant gratitude for their advice, support, and encouragement during the seven-year period over which the research discussed here has evolved. First, I would like to thank my mentors who pointed the way and underscored the need for a psychology of naturalistic settings: Harold Raush and George Levinger at the University of Massachusetts, Harold Proshansky and William Ittelson at the City University of New York, and Ira Iscoe and Robert Reiff at the University of Texas. Next, special thanks are due to Rudolf Moos, who, as editor of this series in Social Ecology, has provided invaluable direction and assistance in preparing this book. Additional thanks for advice in formulating the initial plan of the book are due to Walter Stephan and Carole Holahan. I am also grateful to those individuals who provided assistance in conducting the original research discussed here: Harold Raush, my dissertation advisor for the research discussed in Chapter 5; Susan Saegert and William Ittelson for their suggestions in preparing the analysis reported in Chapter 4; Walter Stephan and Robert Helmreich for their advice in preparing an earlier version of Chapter 7; Arlene Gehring for her assistance in collecting the field data discussed in Chapter 2; Robert Cooke and Saul Rotman for their cooperation in utilizing the field sites discussed in Chapters 5 and 3 respectively. The original research discussed in four chapters was conducted with collaborators, and they deserve special thanks for their role in the development of the research discussed here: Carole Holahan (Chapter 8), Mirilia Bonnes Dobrowolny (Chapter 9), Brian Wilcox (Chapter 3), and Karl Slaikeu (Chapter 6). I am also grateful to Seymour Weingarten and Harvey Graveline at Plenum who have shared with me the burden of making the book a reality. Gratitude of a special kind is due Carole Holahan, whose presence as colleague, collaborator, and spouse imbues all of this work.

Charles J. Holahan

Acknowledgments: The following chapters are based on extensive revisions of work previously published in the following sources: **Chapter 2** • Holahan, C. J. Environmental effects on outdoor social behavior in low-income urban neighborhoods: A naturalistic investigation. *Journal of Applied Social Psychology*, 1976, *6*, 48–63.   **Chapter 4** • Holahan, C. J. Environmental change in a psychiatric setting: A social systems analysis. *Human Relations*, 1976, *29*, 153–166.   **Chapter 5** • Holahan, C. J. Seating patterns and patient behavior in an experimental dayroom. *Journal of Abnormal Psychology*, 1972, *80*, 115–125.   **Chapter 6** • Holahan, C. J. and Slaikeu, K. A. Effects of contrasting degrees of privacy on client self-disclosure in a counseling setting. *Journal of Counseling Psychology*, 1977, *24*, 55–59.   **Chapter 9** • Holahan, C. J. and Dobrowolny, M. B. Cognitive and behavioral correlates of the spatial environment: An interactional analysis. *Environment and Behavior*, 1978.

Contents

CHAPTER 3

Social Coping and Environmental Satisfaction in a
    University Megadorm 45

CHAPTER 4

Coping with Environmental Change: A Social Systems
    Model 57

CHAPTER 7

The Unresponsive Urbanite: Personal versus Situational Determinants

PART III

ENVIRONMENTAL SCHEMATIZATION

Environment
and
Behavior
A Dynamic Perspective

CHAPTER 1

Emergence of a New Perspective

Winston Churchill once remarked, "First we shape our buildings and afterwards our buildings shape us." Churchill was incorrect. Not because people are unaffected by the physical contexts within which they reside; a growing scientific literature affirms, in fact, that they are. Rather Churchill's comment is misleading, for in its compelling simplicity there is implicit an assumption that the effect of environment on behavior is direct, passive, simple, and readily predictable. Nothing could be further from the truth.

During seven years of investigation in the field of environmental psychology, I have been increasingly impressed with the inherently dynamic character of the relationship between environment and behavior. While my research was initially guided by an expectation of a straightforward relationship between context and activity, I found myself engaged eventually in the study of an enthralling human drama. The effect of environment on human behavior, instead of appearing direct, emerged as mediated by a diversity of adaptive maneuvers and stratagems. The human processes involved were dramatically active rather than passive. They were not simple but instead were intricate, subtle, and complex. And, anything but readily predictable, human activity in environmental contexts presented itself as constantly creative and surprising.

This book presents an analysis of the relationship between environment and behavior from such a "dynamic" perspective. Our accent will be on people, and the active and exciting ways in which they deal with environmental challenges. Our view of the role of the human organism in the environment–behavior system will be a positive one, emphasizing the healthy and adaptive ways in which people cope with environmental demands. Our analytical methods and measures will be sufficiently flexible to reflect the multilevel complexity and richness with which individuals relate to the physical environment. And the scope of our inquiry will be broad enough to encompass the often quite unexpected and surprising ways in which human beings respond to environmental circumstances.

Although the orientation of this book encourages a fresh perspective in viewing environment–behavior relationships, the intellectual roots of the research reported here are firmly planted in the soil of environmental psychology. The guiding social values, investigative concerns, and methodological rubrics underlying the present work are shared with that developing field. An adequate evaluation of the thrust of this book requires an appreciation of the historical and disciplinary context out of which it evolved. Therefore, the first part of this chapter presents a discussion of some of the central characteristics of the field of environmental psychology that are mirrored in this book. The last part of the chapter then offers an explication of the dynamic perspective, and of the ways in which it reaches beyond the traditional investigative emphases of environmental psychology.

The chapter is not intended to provide a comprehensive review of environmental psychology but rather a discussion of those aspects of environmental psychology that bear particular relevance to the perspective presented here. Readers who desire, in addition, a comprehensive view of environmental psychology are referred to excellent introductory texts by Proshansky, Ittelson, and Rivlin (1970), Ittelson, Proshansky, Rivlin, and Winkel (1974), and Stokols (1976). In addition, Altman (1975) offers an important theoretical discussion of developments in environmental psychology in the areas of privacy, personal space, territoriality, and crowding.

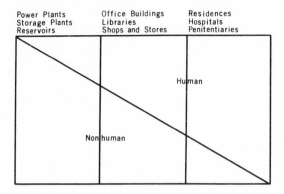

Figure 1. The field of design (Izumi, 1965).

THE HUMAN DIMENSION IN ARCHITECTURE

A fundamental premise behind investigation in the field of environment and behavior involves the assumption of a systematic interrelationship between architecture and patterns of human behavior. Izumi (1965) offers a diagram useful in understanding the meshing of human and nonhuman components in the architectural fabric. Imagine a rectangle (Figure 1) to represent environmental design as related to buildings, with a diagonal separating the human and nonhuman factors. At the left are buildings designed essentially to contain objects, machinery, equipment, and other inanimate objects. At the right are buildings designed solely to contain human beings, as, for example, nursing homes, penitentiaries, psychiatric hospitals, and housing in general. Between these extremes are buildings used to contain both people and objects in varying proportions. These include libraries, laboratories, stores, and offices. As we move from left to right in the diagram, the evaluation of buildings becomes progressively more weighted toward performance as a social setting and against exclusively visually aesthetic properties (Deasy, 1970; Sommer, 1969).

Proshansky *et al.* (1970) affirm that each particular architectural setting has associated with it characteristic patterns of behavior. These activity patterns are consistent and enduring over time regardless of the particular individuals involved in the setting. These authors add, however, that common sense is often a poor guide to appreciating the specific relationship between design and behavior, and that an empirical assessment of the actual performance of architectural settings will often prove both surprising and instructive. Finally, they note that even when we are dramatically affected by the physical settings within which we live, we typically remain unaware of and insensitive to such environmental influences. In fact, Sommer (1972) exhorts investigators in the field of environmental psychology to adopt as a major objective the training of environmental users to be more consciously aware of the pervasive influence exerted by the built environment in daily life. This goal is especially important because so many contemporary buildings fail to achieve behavioral requirements, and of all the types of information on which architectural decisions rely, the category of activity is often the most deficient (Watson, 1970). Bouterline (1970) has asserted, "The dominant situation in modern life is individuals living in a setting which was not built for them" (p. 496).

The nature of the intermeshing of architecture and activity is disturbingly complex. Michelson (1970) offers a frame of reference useful in conceptually unifying the diversity of variables involved in examining the "goodness of fit" between people and the settings in which they reside. The integrating aspect of Michelson's model is the notion of *intersystem congruence*, which describes the degree of match or mismatch between the built environment and a number of other systems, including the cultural, social, and personality systems. In general, the model proposes that "states of variables in one system [coexist] better with states of variables in another system than with other alternative states" (p. 26). After an exhaustive survey of earlier work in the urban environment, Michelson concludes that particular characteristics of urban physical settings emerge as congruent with and supportive of some social processes and incongruent and disruptive of others.

IN SEARCH OF NEW KNOWLEDGE

While the enterprise of constructing physical shelters dates to earliest history, only very recently has society demonstrated a concern about the human impact of the built environment. In the mid-1960s, a small handful of architects and designers, realizing the need for a broadened appreciation of the social and psychological dimensions implicit in the architectural endeavor, turned hopefully toward the behavioral sciences for answers (Sanoff & Cohn, 1970). Answers were few, for behavioral scientists concerned traditionally with human responses to the social environment rather than the physical one were slow to respond (Winkel, 1970). Psychologists particularly proved initially reluctant to guide their research in this new direction (Wohlwill, 1970). Disillusioned architects discovered that acquired scientific facts typically described low-order psychophysiological reactions to extreme environments unlikely to be encountered by practicing environmental designers (Dyckman, 1966; Ventre, 1966). In fact, we knew considerably more about the human response to submarine and space capsule environments than we did of reactions to the suburban environment (Blackman, 1966).

Persistent pressure from the design professions along with increasing societal concern about environmental issues, however, generated a significant change in this state of affairs. The ensuing decade saw a growing number of investigators from a diversity of disciplinary backgrounds, including psychology, geography, sociology, architecture, and planning, joining together in the developing field of environmental psychology. The Environmental Design Research Association, a hybrid professional organization reflecting the disciplinary diversity of researchers in the "environment and behavior" field, was established. A new journal, *Environment and Behavior*, offered a forum for this new area of research endeavor. Universities across the country instituted courses in environmental psychology. The American Psychological Association formed a task force to study concerns in this new area of environment and behavior. Environmental psychology was born.

ASSESSING THE IMPACT OF THE BUILT
ENVIRONMENT

A central thrust of research in environmental psychology has concerned a functionally based analysis of the performance of architectural settings. Our commonsense notions of the relationship between architecture and activity are often erroneous. For example, empirically based evaluations in hospital settings have demonstrated that bedrooms serve a wide range of personal needs in addition to sleeping, dining rooms are used more for social games than eating, and dayrooms are typified more by sleeping than recreation (Proshansky et al., 1970). Thus, an adequate appreciation of the human impact of architectural settings needs to be founded on a systematic empirical evaluation. Environmental research involving this type of assessment has been conducted in a range of different settings and has focused particularly on institutional settings, the urban environment, microinterpersonal behavior, and crowding.

Institutional Settings

Investigations of the psychological impact of institutional environments have tended to focus on psychiatric hospitals and university settings — possibly because both provide captive populations! Researchers in New York City documented higher levels of social activity in a private psychiatric hospital as compared to a municipal and a state hospital (Ittelson, Proshansky, & Rivlin, 1970b). Employing a field experiment in a Saskatchewan hospital, investigators demonstrated marked increases in ward socializing through altering furniture arrangements from a highly unsocial to a more social pattern (Sommer & Ross, 1958). Another New York study led to the interesting finding that semiprivate hospital bedrooms facilitate a wider diversity of usage patterns than do multibed rooms (Ittelson, Proshansky, & Rivlin 1970a).

As high-rise housing has been increasingly utilized for university residence halls, some early findings have pointed to less cooperation, social responsibility, and friendliness in high-rise as opposed to low-rise student housing (Baron, Mandel, Adams, & Griffen, 1976; Bickman, Teger, Gabriele, McLaughlin, Berger, & Sunaday, 1973; Valins & Baum, 1973). The most extensive investigation of the environmental psychology of student housing was conducted by Van der Ryn and Silverstein (1967) at the University of California at Berkeley. It involved an effort to explain excessively high vacancy rates in newly constructed high-rise towers by comparing user needs with existing environmental design. Wheeler (1968) investigated the behavioral consequences of the double-loaded corridor traditionally used in residence halls. His results suggested the benefits of a design alternative involving separating the two sides of the corridor by a central lounge–study area, which would eliminate much of the noise generally encountered in corridors while also affording a setting where students from both sides might interact socially.

The Urban Environment

A second research thrust has concerned the evaluation of urban regions in terms of their spatial "legibility" or clarity as reflected in residents' "cognitive maps" of the city. Though cognitive maps can be generated through a range of verbal or graphic mediums, the predominant technique has been through map drawing (Stea & Downs, 1970). The seminal work in this area was conducted by Lynch (1960), who collected cognitive maps of Boston, Jersey City, and Los Angeles. A series of later studies have followed Lynch's lead and gathered cognitive maps of a number of cities throughout the world — Amsterdam, Rotterdam, and The Hague (de Jonge, 1962), Chicago (Saarinen, 1971), Ciudad Guayana (Appleyard, 1970, 1973), Milan and Rome (Francescato and Mebane, 1973).

Microinterpersonal Behavior

Altman (1975) has proposed the term "microinterpersonal" to identify a level of analysis in environmental psychology focusing on how small social groups are affected by the physical environment in face-to-face interaction. Altman includes in his analysis not only the effect of environment on behavior but also the active ways people use the environment to shape social process. Osmond (1957), in discussing the social quality of physical spaces, defined as "sociofugal" facilities such as hospitals, railway stations, jails, and hotels, which prevent or discourage the development of enduring interpersonal relationships. In contrast, he defined as "sociopetal" those spaces such as tepees, igloos, and Zulu kralls that encourage or foster the growth of stable interpersonal relationships. A number of researchers have been particularly concerned with the use made of space by individuals engaged in conversation; they have studied what have been called "the limits of comfortable conversation." Sommer (1965, 1967, 1969) has demonstrated in a variety of settings that individuals interacting at tables prefer corner-to-corner and face-to-face seating arrangements to side-by-side arrangements. Mehrabian and Diamond (1971) demonstrated in an experimental setting that side-by-side seating was clearly detrimental to conversation. Face-to-face conversation becomes difficult, however, when the distance between partici- pants exceeds a certain limit — Sommer (1961) refers to this limit as 5.5 feet while Hall (1969) indicates 7 feet.

Crowding

While research investigating crowding in laboratory animals has yielded consistent evidence that excessive crowding leads to severe social abnormalities (Calhoun, 1962, 1966), investigations of crowding in human beings present an equivocal and rather complex picture. Stokols (1976) distinguishes between density, the physical limitation of space, and crowding, the individual's experience or perception of restricted space. He defines crowding as the subjective experience that one's demand for space exceeds the supply, and notes that social and personal variables are of importance as well as spatial ones. Altman (1975) sees the break- down in the individual's ability via interpersonal boundary mechanisms to achieve a desired level of privacy as central to the experience of crowding. Wicker (1973), relying on Barker's (1968) theory of behavior settings, has proposed the concept of "over-manning" to explain crowding. Overmanning describes the situation in which the number of persons in a particular social setting exceeds the available social roles. Freedman (1975) has *teenagers* contended that the effects of crowding may not always be negative. He believes that situations of crowding tend to exaggerate what- *rock concerts* ever psychological processes happen to be occurring in the setting → already, and that these processes may be either psychologically *street fairs* positive or negative.

markets
well-museum

A WORKING DEFINITION OF ENVIRONMENTAL PSYCHOLOGY

Clearly environmental psychology represents a very broad sphere of inquiry, and, in fact, the character of this new field is continuing to evolve. Thus, any definition of environmental psychology needs to be general enough to encompass both the breadth and changing nature of the field. With these concerns in mind, we may state: environmental psychology is an evolving area of applied psychology whose focus of investigation is the interrelationship between the physical environment and human behavior and $B = f(p, e)$ experience. While the bulk of research in environmental psychology has concerned the human impact of the built or architectural environment, increasing interest is being directed toward research questions that transcend specific environments, such as crowding and privacy. Because environmental psychology evolved in response to serious societal concerns, it tends to focus on socially relevant problems, to emphasize the applicability of its research findings, and to maintain a molar or holistic level of analysis. Finally, the label *psychology* is employed in a problem definition sense rather than a disciplinary one, for since its inception the field of environmental psychology has reflected an exceptionally broad multidisciplinary involvement.

PLACING PERSPECTIVE IN PERSPECTIVE

The research program presented in this book is rooted in the traditional concerns of environmental psychology. The issues investigated here are direct responses to pressing social concerns. The studies discussed offer examples of work in the areas of behavioral mapping, cognitive mapping, and proxemics. The settings investigated are like those many other environmental psychologists have studied, and include institutions, open space settings, and the urban environment. What is unique about this book is the manner in which environmental psychology is approached. It is this approach to the field of environmental psychology that reflects the dynamic perspective.

A perspective in general refers not to the subject matter or content of a scientific discipline but rather to the way in which a field of inquiry *approaches* the phenomena it studies. A perspective shapes, for example, the kinds of questions an investigator asks, and how and where appropriate answers are sought. The importance of reflecting seriously on the way in which we approach our subject should not be underestimated, especially for a young and still impressionable field like environmental psychology. The manner in which we approach the environment–behavior system limits from the outset the type of answers to be found. Our perspective colors the kinds of data we seek, are willing to accept, or are inclined to ignore. In addition, precisely because a perspective is abstract, subtle, and implicit, it is particularly difficult to recognize and identify its pervasive underlying influence in the scientific enterprise.

A DYNAMIC PERSPECTIVE

The dynamic perspective advanced in this book encourages two stances in terms of how environmental psychology might approach its subject matter. First, it emphasizes that environmental psychology should focus its investigative attention on those *human processes* that *mediate* the effects of environment on behavior.

Second, it underscores the importance of focusing particular interest on the positive and adaptive ways in which people *cope* with environmental challenges. The thrust of the dynamic perspective encourages viewing the human response to environmental circumstances as inherently *active, varied,* and *creative.* This orientation differs from that which has tended to characterize investigation in environmental psychology in two important respects.

First, research in the field of environmental psychology has typically been focused on the "input" and "output" ends of the environment–behavior equation. In terms of input, attention has been directed toward developing a taxonomy or lexicon of features of the physical environment that influence particular types of activity. With regard to output, research has been focused on the development and application of measurement techniques responsive to behavioral variations between contrasting environmental settings. This tendency in environmental psychology to focus on specific design dimensions and their functional impacts has been shaped by the discipline's close ties to the design professions. In fact, this orientation has facilitated environmental psychology's providing a considerable amount of design-relevant information to practicing designers. The dynamic perspective emphasizes the need to examine, in addition, the range of human processes that mediate the link between input (physical context) and output (activity).

Second, the manner in which environmental psychologists have traditionally posed their research questions has resulted in a body of environmental knowledge that tends to imply that a passive human organism is acted upon by an overwhelming environmental context. This orientation in environmental psychology has resulted from an effort to apply the notion of behavioral prediction from behavioral science directly to the study of environment and behavior. This approach has facilitated both the accumulation of an impressive data base in environmental psychology and a high level of professional respect for the new field in the scientific community. The dynamic perspective encourages a broadening of this orientation to include, in addition, a full appreciation of the

reading on subways/ busses

active, positive coping strategies people engage in when confronted by environmental difficulties. It is precisely because such human coping is often both highly creative and quite surprising that it defies easy behavioral prediction.

AGENDA FOR THIS BOOK

With these concerns in mind, this book has been written for two purposes. First, it is an effort to afford a fuller knowledge base in environmental psychology of some of the active and positive ways in which people cope with environmental demands. The major portion of the book consists of three sections, each detailing a different human process that reflects a dynamic perspective in terms of the human relationship to the environment. The book's first section describes the process of *environmental coping* evidenced when people deal actively and positively with environmental challenges. Section II discusses the subtle and surprising behavioral adjustments or *accommodations* in which people engage when badly designed environmental settings lead to undesirable social consequences. The final section examines the active role people play in imposing personal meaning and significance on their images or *schemata* of the physical environment.

A second goal of the book is to encourage other investigators in the field of environmental psychology to consider the relevance of such a dynamic perspective to their own research endeavors. An effort has been made to include a number of diverse research studies as supporting evidence for the position advanced here, and it is hoped these will afford a sufficient data base for the reader to personally evaluate the merit of the viewpoint suggested. The separate research studies are presented in such a way that the process of discovery by which the dynamic perspective originally emerged remains evident. Finally, the book's last chapter presents an explicit discussion of the relevance of the dynamic perspective to environmental psychology's future development.

REFERENCES

Altman, I. *The Environment and social behavior: Privacy, personal space, territory and crowding.* Monterey, California: Brooks / Cole, 1975.

Appleyard, D. Styles and methods of structuring a city. *Environment and Behavior,* 1970, *2,* 199–218.

Appleyard, D. 'Notes on urban perception and knowledge.' In R. M. Downs & D. Stea, (Eds.), *Image and environment.* Chicago: Aldine, 1973.

Barker, R. *Ecological psychology: Concepts and methods for studying the environment of human behavior.* Stanford: Stanford University Press, 1968.

Baron, R. M., Mandel, D. R., Adams, C. A., & Griffen, L. M. Effects of social density in university residential environments. *Journal of Personality and Social Psychology,* 1976, *34,* 434–466.

Bickman, L., Teger, A., Gabriele, T., McLaughlin, C., Berger, M., & Sunaday, E. Dormitory density and helping behavior. *Environment and Behavior,* 1973, *5,* 465–490.

Blackman, A. Scientism and planning. *The American Behavioral Scientist,* 1966, *10,* 24–28.

Boutourline, S. The concept of environmental management. In H. M. Proshansky, W. H. Ittelson, & L. G. Rivlin, (Eds.), *Environmental pyschology: Man and his physical setting.* New York: Holt, Rinehart & Winston, 1970.

Calhoun, J. B. Population density and social pathology. *Scientific American,* 1962, *206,* 139–146.

Calhoun, J. B. The role of space in animal sociology. *Journal of Social Issues,* 1966, *22,* 46–59.

Deasy, C. M. When architects consult people. *Psychology Today,* 1970, *3,* 54–57, 78–79.

de Jonge, D. Images of urban areas, their structures and psychological foundations. *Journal of the American Institute of Planners,* 1962, *28,* 266–276.

Dyckman, J. W. Environment and behavior: Introduction. *The American Behavioral Scientist,* 1966, *10,* 1–2.

Francescato, D., & Mebane, W. How citizens view two great cities: Milan and Rome. In R. M. Downs & D. Stea, (Eds.), *Image and environment.* Chicago: Aldine, 1973, pp. 131–147.

Freedman, J. L. *Crowding and human behavior.* San Francisco: Freeman, 1975.

Hall, E. T. *The hidden dimension.* New York: Doubleday, 1969.

Ittelson, W. H., Proshansky, H. M., & Rivlin, L. G. Bedroom size and social interaction of the psychiatric ward. *Environment and behavior,* 1970, *2,* 255–270(a).

Ittelson, W. H., Proshansky, H. M., & Rivlin, L. G. The environmental psychology of the psychiatric ward. In H. M. Proshansky, W. H. Ittelson, & L. G. Rivlin (Eds.), *Environmental psychology: Man and his physical setting.* New York: Holt, Rhinehart, & Winston, 1970(b).

Ittelson, W., Proshansky, H., Rivlin, L., & Winkel, G. *An introduction to environmental psychology.* New York: Holt, Rinehart & Winston, 1974.

Izumi, K. Psychosocial phenomena and building design. *Building Research*, 1965, *2*, 9–11.

Lynch, K. *The image of the city.* Cambridge, Massachusetts: M.I.T. Press, 1960.

Mehrabian, A., & Diamond, S. Seating arrangement and conversation. *Sociometry*, 1971, *34*, 281–289.

Michelson, W. *Man and his urban environment: A sociological approach.* Reading, Massachussetts: Addison-Wesley, 1970.

Osmond, H. Function as the basis of psychiatric ward design. *Mental Hospitals*, 8, 1957, 23–30.

Proshansky, H. M., Ittelson, & Rivlin, L. Freedom of choice and behavior in a physical setting. In H. M. Proshansky, W. Ittelson, & L. Rivlin (Eds.), *Environmental psychology: Man and his physical setting.* New York: Holt, Rinehart & Winston, 1970.

Proshansky, H. M., Ittelson, W. H., & Rivlin, L. G. (Eds.). *Environmental psychology: Man and his physical setting.* New York: Holt, Rinehart & Winston, 1970.

Saarinen, T. F. *The use of projective techniques in geographic research.* Paper presented at Environment and Cognition Conference, City University of New York, Graduate Center, June 1971.

Sanoff, H., & Cohn, S. Preface. In H. Sanoff & S. Cohn, (Eds.), *Proceedings of the first annual environmental design research association conference.* Raleigh: North Carolina State University, 1970.

Sommer, R. Leadership and group geography. *Sociometry.* 1961, *24*, 99–110.

Sommer, R. *Design awareness.* New York: Holt, Rinehart & Winston, 1972.

Sommer, R. Further studies of small group ecology. *Sociometry.* 1965, *28*, 337–348.

Sommer, R. Small group ecology. *Psychological Bulletin*, 1967, *67*, 145–152.

Sommer, R. *Personal space: The behavioral basis of design.* Englewood Cliffs, New Jersey: Prentice-Hall, 1969.

Sommer, R. & Ross, H. Social interaction on a geriatrics ward. *International Journal of Social Psychiatry*, 1958, *4*, 128–133.

Stea, D., & Downs, R. M. From the outside looking in at the inside looking out. *Environment and Behavior*, 1970, *2*, 3–12.

Stokols, D. (Ed.). *Psychological perspectives on environment and behavior: Theory, research and applications.* New York: Plenum Press, 1976.

Stokols, D. The experience of crowding in primary and secondary environments. *Environment and Behavior*, 1976, *8*, 49–86.

Valins, S., & Baum, A. Residential group size, social interaction, and crowding. *Environment and Behavior*, 1973, *5*, 421–439.

Van der Ryn, S., & Silverstein, M. *Dorms at Berkeley.* New York: Educational Facilities Laboratories, 1967.

Ventre, F. T. Toward a science of environment. *The American Behavioral Scientist*, 1966, *10*, 28–31.

Watson, D. Modeling the activity system. In H. Sanoff & S. Cohn (Eds.), *Proceedings of the 1st annual environmental design research association conference*. Raleigh: North Carolina State University, 1970.

Wheeler, L. *Behavioral research for architectural planning and design*. Terre Haute, Indiana: Ewing Miller Associates, 1968.

Wicker, A. Undermanning theory and research: Implications for the study of psychological and behavioral effects of excess population. *Representative Research in Social Psychology*, 1973, *4*, 185–206.

Winkel, G. The nervous affair between behavior scientists and designers. *Psychology Today*, 1970, *3*, 31–35; 74.

Wohlwill, J. The emerging discipline of environmental psychology. *American Psychologist*, 1970, *25*, 303–312.

PART I

ENVIRONMENTAL COPING

ENVIRONMENTAL COPING

An office worker in Los Angeles embarks 30 minutes early for work each morning in anticipation of freeway traffic congestion. A university sophomore jogs between classes on a scattered and fragmented midwestern campus. An elderly New Yorker walks slowly home by a circuitous route where jostling by active youngsters will be avoided. Each of these cases reflects human coping efforts pitted against challenging environmental circumstances. Coping with environmental demands like these has, in fact, become commonplace in contemporary life. If we reflect for a moment on the "hassles" that are a predictable aspect of our daily lives, it becomes evident that many of these involve environmental impediments in our homes and neighborhoods, in the places we work, and in traffic and pedestrian settings.

Less apparent, yet of particular significance to the environmental psychologist, are the ways in which people learn to cope with the depersonalizing and socially isolating character of so many of the environmental settings that are familiar features of modern life. While this type of coping is more subtle than dealing with the physical demands of the environment, it represents a fundamental aspect of the environmental coping process because too often even the best of contemporary design is out of step with human needs at the level of social and psychological functioning. Consider, for example, the new urban neighborhoods of faceless high-rise structures that inhibit rather than support one's sense of social identity and group belongingness; the megadorms increasingly employed in "progressive" university housing, which choke the prospect of meaningful social participation at a human scale; the efficient hospital settings whose only "therapy" is to foster feelings of separateness and isolation. In this section, we will examine some of the coping processes that environmental users engage in when confronted by challenges to the quality of social life in a range of environmental contexts like these.

When I initially approached the study of the settings reported in this section, my intention was to document the negative consequences of poor behavioral design. I discovered instead the fascinating ways in which people manage through environmental coping to offset the potentially negative effects of unsuitable environmental settings. We will see that such environmental coping presents one of the most exciting and compelling of the human processes that mediate the environment–behavior link. For through environmental coping, individuals evolve a range of adaptive behavioral strategies that succeed in converting potentially dehumanizing environmental settings into ones characterized instead by positive and effective social interchange. Here we are spectators to the drama of human resilience and determination prevailing over environmental constraint.

FIELD STUDIES

The research studies reported in this section were conducted in three different environmental settings, which through previous speculation had been identified as especially serious failures in their performance as human habitats. They include a high-rise public housing project, a university megadorm, and a psychiatric ward in a large municipal hospital. The studies have been selected to reflect considerable diversity in terms of the physical environments studied, the characteristics of the subject samples, and the nature of the research methodology.

The purpose of the research in this section is to afford an initial, empirically sound portrait of life in such environmental contexts. Because it is important that such an initial picture be relatively free of experimental distortion, the research strategies here will reflect an effort to achieve a naturalistic and holistic impression. In Section II, where our investigative concerns will be more narrowly focused, we will introduce a greater level of experimental control. The type of empirical evaluation involved in these field studies assumes an added significance when we recognize that in each of these settings the adverse psychological consequences were wholly unanticipated by the generally progressive and innovative planners who sponsored their development.

Chapter 2 describes environmental coping in a low-income community, where residents accustomed to a rich and varied street life are confronted with the stagnating landscape of high-rise public housing. Using a naturalistic procedure, the study involves the behavioral mapping of outdoor activity in the neighborhood in an effort to empirically record how a low-income population is affected by and copes with the environmental demands of high-rise public housing. We will see that tenants usurp any usable nook in the outdoor environment to support their established social needs. Children claim a deserted amphitheater for group play, while an adjacent modernistic playground sits vacant. Adults engaged in casual social banter congregate on city stoops, ignoring a neighborhood park located a block away. While these residents are powerless to alter physically their neighborhood setting, they are able to redefine the function of available outdoor space to conform with existing social demands. Thus, spaces designed initially for nonsocial functional tasks can be reclaimed by community members to perform informally as casual social settings.

In Chapter 3, we observe college students in a dissatisfying high-rise megadorm evolve coping strategies to counteract the deleterious environmental influences. The study involves a survey of students' dissatisfactions in the megadorm setting, along with an effort to document how social coping strategies evolve in response to the environmental pressures. We will see that in order to deal with the social ambiguity and fragmentation of the megadorm, residents develop friendship patterns that are spatially proximate and readily accessible. Employing an "interactional" framework, the study will also investigate individual differences in the development of environmental coping strategies. Quite interestingly, we will discover that the type of coping that evolves varies with and is appropriate to the particular student's level of social competence.

Chapter 4 involves a field experiment and documents a fascinating process of environmental coping by psychiatric hospital staff, who are forced to deal with the social disruption of a large-scale ward remodeling. The study employs a number of converging experimental measures, including behavioral mapping, informal naturalistic observation, and open-ended interviews, to gather a full and rich portrait of how hospital staff respond to an environmental change that implies concomitant shifts in the ward's social structure. Here we will conceptualize environmental coping in the framework of a social systems model, following the staff's response to environmental change as it evolves through a series of clearly demarcated temporal phases. Particularly important is a process of "personalization," whereby environmental users assimilate the design changes imposed by outsiders into their personal psychological framework of relating to the hospital environment.

DYNAMIC ASPECTS OF ENVIRONMENTAL COPING

Because the chapters in this section are quite diversified in terms of both the environments studied and the research methodologies employed, it will be valuable at the outset to note some basic similarities in the environmental coping process as it occurs in each instance. Three features of environmental coping reflect its essentially dynamic nature: (1) it is an active human process, (2) it reflects a high level of personal resourcefulness, and (3) it is characterized by individual differences.

Active

Environmental coping is foremost an active, human-initiated process. In it we see individuals assume an active and positive stance in evolving a range of adaptive behavioral maneuvers and stratagems in dealing with potentially negative environmental threats. In this sense environmental coping represents a process of *assimilation*, whereby environmental users successfully incorporate the surrounding physical context into the ongoing pattern of their social needs and social activity. Residents of the public housing project manage to reclaim spaces originally designed for nonsocial functional tasks to meet their continuing informal social needs. Students in the megadorm initiate a pattern of proximate friendship networks to counteract the antisocial influences of the physical setting. Staff members on the remodeled psychiatric ward, after initially resisting the change effort, become positively involved in the remodeling by gaining a sense of personal control in the change process.

Resourcefulness

Environmental coping is, in addition, characterized by a high level of personal resourcefulness, determination, and even creativity. It is exhilarating to observe the level of determination and endurance behind a group's effort to bring an environment into line with its social needs. The degree of creativity apparent in the diversity of coping strategies that environmental users evolve, and especially in the appropriateness of a particular coping response to a specific environmental challenge, is both surprising and enlightening. In the public housing environment, where the existing design fails to afford essential informal social space, coping occurs at the level of spatial behavior and involves a functional redefinition of available space. In the megadorm, coping involves the evolution of friendship networks that compensate for the socially fragmenting influences of the environment. On the psychiatric ward, coping develops on a psychological plane, since the effects of the environmental change are experienced as a psychological threat to the staff's sense of autonomy and control in the sphere of role behavior.

Individual Differences

Another and especially interesting aspect of environmental coping is the extent to which coping strategies are individually tailored to the unique needs, experiences, and skills of the persons engaged in the coping process. In each of the chapters in this section, we will see that different people evolve different and unique tactics in dealing with environmental challenges, and that these strategies are suited to personal abilities and personal styles of action. In the housing project, youths and adults demonstrate very different response patterns to the project environment, which are consistent with the differing functional needs of the two groups. In the university housing environment, we will see that the style of coping that develops is congruent with students' levels of social competence. In the hospital setting, each echelon of ward staff responds differentially to the environmental changes as a function of its unique needs. The concept of "person–environment fit," which has recently begun to gain prominence in psychology as a model of psychological adjustment, is appropriate here, although it assumes a somewhat different meaning. From this perspective, "fit" is envisioned not in the traditional homeostatic sense but rather as a dynamic, individually managed, actively maintained balance that is altered as people and circumstances change.

CHAPTER 2

Street Life and High-Rise Public Housing

A remarkable and quite neglected form of street theater plays each day in the heart of the central city. It pits the coping efforts of inner-city residents against the inexorable transformation of the urban ghetto. Gradually, the old tenement neighborhood boasting a robust social life is being replaced by high-rise housing projects distinguished instead by social isolation. Jacobs (1961) describes eloquently the vivid contrast between the social vitality of the ghetto and the psychological barrenness of the new high-rise projects. The Pruitt-Igoe houses in St. Louis, which were hailed as a modern design achievement, have become notorious for their almost total failure to function effectively at a social psychological level (Rainwater, 1968; Yancy, 1971). Newman (1972) has recently documented the consistent relationship between low social cohesion and high crime level typical in high-rise public housing. Gans (1962) has concluded that too often the physical changes of urban renewal fail to substantially improve the lives of the poor.

In a systematic study in Puerto Rico, Hollingshead and Rogler (1963) studied two groups of families, one of which had recently moved into a new government housing project and the other of which had remained in the ghetto. They found that while over 60% of the ghetto dwellers liked living in the ghetto, over three-quarters of the persons relocated in the housing project were unhappy with their new living conditions. Hollingshead and Rogler concluded that housing meeting the standards of city planners and architects and built by an enlightened government may still result in unacceptable social conditions. Fried (1963) has reported a study of forced relocation of low-income residents in Boston's West End. He found that residents suffered a severe grief reaction, which showed features similar to mourning for a lost person and which for many individuals persisted as long as two years. He concluded that forced dislocation from an urban ghetto is a highly disruptive and disturbing experience, characterized by clear expressions of grief and potential danger to mental health for many people.

THE SOCIAL FABRIC OF THE GHETTO

Common to these studies is evidence that the urban ghetto is a stable social unit. Fried and Gleicher (1970) describe the ghetto area as the region in which an immense and interrelated set of social networks is localized. Fried (1963) notes that the expressions of grief associated with forced relocation are intimately related to the pattern and conditions of social relationships in the ghetto. He writes that "they cannot 'drop in' as casually as before, they do not have the sense of being surrounded by a familiar area and familiar people . . . the changes do involve important elements of stability and continuity in their lives." Hollingshead and Rogler (1963) stress that the central reason the residents of the government housing project in their study disliked their new housing was that it lacked the comfortable and informal contact with neighbors characteristic of the ghetto.

At issue are contrasting basic assumptions concerning the relationship between urban design and human behavior. Typically, modern designers have favored a visually simple environment, while behavioral scientists interested in design problems have preferred a functionally complex one. While both parties favor order in the urban environment, conceptions of what type of order is needed differ sharply. The designer, for example, strives to create

order on a purely visual scale. Such visually oriented designs tend
to spatially separate diverse types of behavior. Jacobs (1961) has
sternly criticized this approach to urban design: "To approach a
city, or even a city neighborhood, as if it were a larger architectural
problem, capable of being given order by converting it into a
disciplined work of art, is to make the mistake of attempting to
substitute art for life." The behavioral scientist, in contrast,
envisions order emerging at a functional level. He tends to favor
mixing diverse types of behavior, allowing them to function in
complementary and mutually supportive ways.

Critics of modern design contend that the emphasis on
simplicity of form has neglected the important social function
played by the outdoor environment in the urban neighborhood.
Design strategies that emphasize screening off diversified
activities from one another in the name of visual aesthetics impede
the rich informal social exchange characteristic of the low-income
neighborhood. Social functions such as communication and group
support in low-income neighborhoods are met through informal
and largely accidental social contact between people pursuing
diversified tasks in public open spaces.

This is not to say that *all* run-down areas are socially well
organized. However, many ghetto areas that have traditionally
been called "disorganized" have with closer investigation shown a
high degree of social organization; although the structure of such
organization differs from that to which middle-class persons are
accustomed. The Italian ghetto studied intensively by Whyte
(1943), for example, demonstrated a clear internal organization,
which had remained unrecognized by outside middle-class
observers. Dotson (1951) showed that although lower-class
persons in New Haven did not frequent voluntary organizations,
they did maintain frequent social contacts with relatives. In a
classic investigation in London's East End, Young and Willmott
(1962) have described the social dependence of wives on their
mothers for interpersonal contact, help-giving, and child care
within the framework of geographically proximate support
networks. Hartman (1963) has written of West End Boston:

> In the West End, and in most working class communities which have
> been reported in the literature, there was considerable interaction
> with the surrounding physical and social environment, an interaction
> which formed an integral part of the lives of the people. . . . Among a
> population for whom sitting on stoops, congregating on street
> corners, hanging out of windows, talking with shopkeepers, and
> strolling in the local area formed a critical part of the *modus vivendi*,
> the concept of personal living space must certainly be expanded to
> include outdoor as well as indoor space.

The physical design of high-rise apartment buildings, in
particular, blocks many of the avenues of social exchange
characteristic of the ghetto. For example, in the ghetto, windows of
tenement houses offer a rich medium through which ghetto
residents can hail passersby or converse casually with neighbors in
adjacent buildings. Also, because local stores are typically scattered
throughout the ghetto neighborhood, residents are brought
naturally within range of the doors and windows of many other
neighbors while pursuing daily errands (Gans, 1962). High-rise
housing, in contrast, is characterized by a minimum of semipublic
space between apartments, and tends to exert an atomizing effect
on informal relationships. Yancy (1971) has noted that families
living in Pruitt-Igoe retreated to the interior of their apartments,
losing the social support and neighborly protection found in other
lower- and working-class neighborhoods. Michelson (1970) in
referring to the work of Rainwater (1968) adds:

> Congruence, however, carries with it the opposite, incongruence. . . .
> Witness the complaints of families with small children who live high
> off the ground in public housing projects. Mothers are not always free
> to follow their children to ground level, where great numbers of them
> frequently roam without supervision. Getting to and from the
> ground requires elevators, which the children often adopt as play
> toys, putting them out of commission. The smaller children often are
> set upon by older bullies, who can find hiding places in areas such as
> stairwells where authorities are hard pressed to control them.

A NATURALISTIC FIELD STUDY

To date, with the exception of a small body of survey research,
almost all of the argument in this area has been highly speculative.

In fact, there have been no empirical data to support the basic contention that high-rise housing projects are characterized by a less social and active outdoor life than is the old ghetto neighborhood. The purpose of this study was to afford such an empirical test. Specifically, the study was designed (1) to measure and compare the level of outdoor socializing across three contrasting urban environments — an old ghetto neighborhood, a traditional high-rise housing project, and a housing project where an innovative design solution was intended to encourage and support street activity; and (2) to develop a behavioral portrait of each of these environments, including both the range of activities that occur in public spaces and some of the environmental features that support street activity. On the basis of previous speculations concerning the relationship between behavior and urban design (Fried & Gleicher, 1970; Gans, 1962; Hartman, 1963; Jacobs, 1961), it was predicted that the old neighborhood and the innovative project would be characterized by higher levels of outdoor social behavior than would the traditional project. It was further anticipated that the old neighborhood and the innovative project would demonstrate outdoor behavioral profiles typified by higher frequencies of recreational and leisure behavior relative to functional or task-oriented activity than would the traditional project.

Three adjacent sites within a low-income, inner-city neighborhood were selected for comparison — an old neighborhood of low-rise tenement houses, a traditional high-rise housing project, and an innovatively designed high-rise housing project. The two projects were comparable in age, project size, and building height. Residents of the three sites were similar in socioeconomic level and racial background. Behavioral measures were collected in each site on three Saturday afternoons during the summer. Measures were of two types: (1) a five-minute time sample of the social behavior of a random sample of 15% of individuals outdoors in each site, and (2) a profile of the range of activities of all individuals outdoors in each site based on a single observation of each individual.

CONTRASTING HOUSING ENVIRONMENTS

The area selected for study was a neighborhood in New York City's Lower East Side, which was low-income, predominantly Puerto Rican and black, and slowly being redeveloped by the city. The old neighborhood site consisted of 5 different blocks randomly selected from the 36-block neighborhood adjacent to the two projects. The old neighborhood was characterized by three- to five-story tenements, built in a row, flush with the sidewalk. Eighty-five percent of buildings in the neighborhood were completed before 1940. While the neighborhood was predominantly residential, occasional commercial establishments, such as grocery stores, candy stores, and cleaners, were mixed in at the street level. Physically the neighborhood met the description of an urban slum. Housing quality varied but tended toward poor condition, with some badly deteriorated buildings and an occasional boarded-up site. Density in the old neighborhood as in both projects ranged from 350 to 400 persons per acre. Median monthly rent in the old neighborhood was $76, compared to $82 in both projects.

The two housing projects were built along the eastern boundary of the old neighborhood and were adjacent to both the old neighborhood and to one another. Both projects were completed in 1959 and were similar in the physical design of project buildings. Each had between 16 and 18 buildings of up to 14 floors. Amount of outdoor space was comparable for both projects and was of a "superblock" nature, i.e., a number of city blocks were included in the project grounds and closed to automobile traffic. The two projects differed markedly, however, in the design of outdoor space. The traditional project, which was typical of most public housing projects, consisted chiefly of grassy areas that were fenced off to prohibit tenant use, a few playgrounds with minimal and badly deteriorated playground equipment, and row benches along the asphalt entranceways. The innovative project boasted a modernistic and aesthetically pleasing outdoor environment, which had been added to the project in 1965 specifically to encourage and support outdoor activity.* The innovative design

*The innovative outdoor environment was designed by architect M. Paul Friedberg.

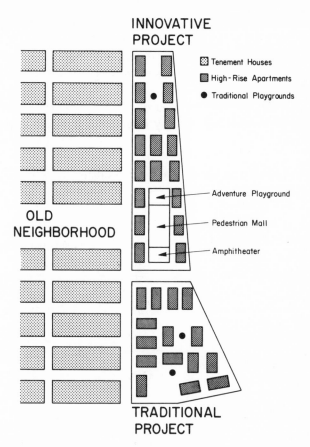

Figure 2. Schematic representation of the three environmental settings.

was restricted to the large central project area and stood in contrast to the standard row benches along the peripheral entranceways. The new design features were of three types: (1) A modernistic adventure playground and wading area, which included creatively designed concrete and timber playground equipment, replaced the old central playground; (2) a red brick-surfaced pedestrian mall surrounded by small groupings of benches and tables was built over the previously closed-off grassy areas; and (3) a large sunken amphitheater was added as a forum for public events. Figure 2 shows a schematic representation of the three environmental settings.

The residents in each environmental setting did not constitute a random assignment of subjects to experimental conditions. Self-selection processes may be assumed to have been of some importance in determining area of residence. The best source of information concerning any systematic differences in resident

Table 1. Characteristics of Residents in Each Environmental Setting from U.S. Census of 1970

Characteristics	Environmental setting		
	Old neighborhood	Traditional project	Innovative project
Race			
White	35	21	16
Black	16	29	24
Spanish mother tongue	49	49	60
Economic level			
Median income	5,128	5,774	5,399
Unemployment (% for 16 years and above)	36	32	33
Families below poverty level	30	25	26
Mobility patterns			
Length of residence			
1965–70	62	34	41
1960–64	18	27	36
1959 or earlier	20	39	23
Previous residence			
New York central city	73	86	88
New York outside central city	2	2	.5
Outside New York	9	3	2.5
Abroad	16	9	9

characteristics between settings is the U.S. Census of 1970, since census tracts correspond almost exactly to the three areas studied. Three types of information are relevant: race, economic level, and mobility patterns. Table 1 summarizes this information for each environmental setting.

The two projects are comparable along all three dimensions, though the traditional project is slightly higher than the innovative project in percentage of whites to nonwhites, median income, and length of residence. Differences between the old neighborhood and the two projects are more pronounced. In the old neighborhood, the percentage of whites to nonwhites is highest and economic level is lowest. While there are no conclusive data relating these variables to street activity, indications are that the influence is probably mixed. While nonwhites are believed to demonstrate a higher level of street activity than whites (Brower, 1973), higher income groups are assumed to show less such activity than lower ones (Hartman, 1963). The most important difference between the old neighborhood and the projects is in mobility patterns. In the old neighborhood, length of residence is shortest, and a higher percentage of residents come from out of the city or abroad. Both these factors tend to militate against social stability in the neighborhood, though their effect on street life is difficult to predict.

BEHAVIOR MAPPING

Outdoor behavior was observed and recorded in each setting using an extension of the behavioral mapping procedure developed by Ittelson, Rivlin, and Proshansky (1970). The behavioral map of each environment consisted of a record of the number of individuals engaged in each of a number of predetermined behavior types in each subarea of the environment. A distinction was made between youths and adults, with youths defined as all persons judged to be below age 20, and adults as all persons age 20 and above. Through initial observation sessions in an adjoining area, a list of behavior categories was selected which covered most of the behavioral variance for the settings studied. In addition to scoring type of behavior, each subject's specific location in the environment was recorded at each observation interval. Observations involved complete coverage of all physical spaces in the selected environments on a time-sampling basis. Observations were recorded on data sheets designed for quick and easy use by observers.

Two specific types of behavioral maps were collected: (1) Individual Social Records (ISR) and (2) Activity Maps (AM). The ISR procedure was designed to compare the *level* of social behavior over environmental settings. A random-number table was used to randomly select 15% of the persons in each site for observation. Then, in a time-sampling procedure, a recording of each subject's behavior was performed at 30-second intervals for a period of up to 10 intervals. Each subject was given a score indicating the percent of his behavior that fell into each of the three following behavior categories. (1) Verbal Interaction — social interaction between two or more persons that included conversation; (2) Nonverbal Interaction — social interaction between two or more persons that did not include conversation. Social behavior included such activities as ball playing, repairing an automobile, sitting in a group, and walking together when these activities clearly involved two or more people in a social grouping. The distinction between verbal and nonverbal was determined by whether or not the individual selected for observation was engaged in conversation (speaking or listening) at the instant his behavior was recorded. (3) Isolation — any activity performed by an individual in isolation, i.e., sitting alone or walking alone.

The AM procedure was designed to compare the *distribution* of a range of activities over environmental settings. It involved an instantaneous recording of the behavior of all subjects in each site, based on a single observation of each individual. Each subject was given a score indicating which of the three following activity categories his behavior fell into: (1) Active Recreation — ball playing, using playground equipment, bike riding; (2) Leisure — sitting, standing, and casual activity, such as listening to a radio; (3) Functional — task-related activity, such as shopping, child care, and repairing an automobile.

Previous research has shown the behavioral mapping

procedure to have high interobserver and split-half reliability
(Ittelson *et al.*, 1970). After training in the specific behavioral
scoring procedures used here, interrater reliability was determined
for the two observers. Agreement exceeded 90% on all measures.

The timing of observations was determined by the desire to
compare the three settings during peak outdoor use. Observations
were conducted by two trainees from CUNY'S Environmental
Psychology Program on three Saturday afternoons from 1:00 to
5:30 during the months of June and July. All observations were
conducted in good weather when the temperature ranged between
75 and 95 degrees. In order to minimize accidentally repeating
observations of the same subject, while at the same time permitting
a sampling of the three settings over time, the following procedure
was developed. Each environment was divided into three equal
physical subareas, and each subarea was observed only once, with a
different subarea being observed each Saturday. Thus, on the first
Saturday of observations, one subarea was observed from each of
the three environments. On the following Saturday, one of the
remaining subareas was observed in each environment, and so on.
The particular subarea to be observed on a given Saturday and the
sequence of observations across environments were determined
randomly. Each observer spent 1½ hours in each of the three sites
during each observation period, resulting in a total of 4½ hours of
observation in each site over the course of the study. The two
observers walked together, proceeding through each subarea by a
preselected route. While one observer employed the ISR
procedure, the other used the AM procedure. Observers carried a
stopwatch and behavior score sheets attached to a clipboard. They
were dressed casually, as were neighborhood residents, and
attempted neither to attract attention nor to interact with
residents.

OUTDOOR SOCIAL ACTIVITY

The total number of subjects observed under the ISR procedure in
the old neighborhood, the traditional project, and the innovative

Table 2. Percent of Behavior in Each Social Behavior Category by Age Group across the Three Environmental Settings

Age group	Behavior category	Environmental setting			ANOVA		
		Old neighborhood	Traditional project	Innovative project	F	df	p
All subjects	Social verbal	63	52	80	4.57	2/122	.01[a]
	Social nonverbal	23	23	6	3.36	2/122	.04[a]
	Isolated	14	25	14	1.33	2/122	.27
Youths	Social verbal	62	53	91	7.10	2/66	.002[a]
	Social nonverbal	32	26	8	3.00	2/66	.06
	Isolated	6	21	1	3.79	2/66	.03[a]
Adults	Social verbal	64	50	61	.58	2/56	.57
	Social nonverbal	16	18	4	.95	2/56	.39
	Isolated	20	32	35	.75	2/56	.48

[a] Significant with $\alpha = .05$.

project was 48, 48, and 29, respectively. Table 2 shows the percent of behavior in each behavior category across the three environmental settings for all subjects and for youths and adults separately, along with the results of the one-way analyses of variance. Let us look first at the data for all subjects. The difference between the three settings was statistically significant at the .01 level for verbal interaction. The Scheffé (1959) multiple-comparison procedure was used to test differences between specific environmental settings. This procedure indicated that there was significantly more verbal interaction in the average of the old neighborhood and innovative project compared to the traditional project as predicted ($F = 7.14$, $df = 2/122$, $p < .05$). Individual comparisons showed that the difference between the innovative and traditional projects was statistically significant ($F = 9.14$, $df = 2/122$, $p < .025$), while the differences between the old neighborhood and either the traditional or the innovative projects were not statistically significant. The Sheffé procedure indicated that there was significantly less nonverbal interaction in the innovative project than in the average of the old neighborhood and the traditional project ($F = 6.71$, $df = 1/122$, $p < .05$), the old neighborhood alone ($F = 5.25$, $df = 2/122$, $p < .10$), or the traditional project alone ($F = 5.64$, $df = 1/122$, $p < .10$). (Scheffé recommends an alpha level of .10 in using his multiple-comparison procedure.) The traditional project showed the highest level of isolated behavior, though this was not statistically significant.

It is revealing to further analyze the ISR data in terms of age. For youths the differences between the three sites were particularly strong, while for adults there were no statistically significant differences over settings. For youths, the differences between settings were statistically significant at the .002 level for verbal interaction, the .03 level for isolation, and approached significance for nonverbal interaction ($p < .06$). The Scheffé multiple-comparison procedure indicated that there was significantly more verbal interaction in the average of the old neighborhood and the innovative project than in the traditional project ($F = 7.72$, $df = 2/66$, $p < .05$). Individual comparisons showed more verbal

interaction in the innovative project than in either the old neighborhood ($F = 6.99$, $df = 2/66$, $p < 05$) or the traditional project
($F = 13.84$, $df = 2/66$, $p < .01$). Nonverbal interaction was again
lowest in the innovative project. Isolated behavior for youths was
highest in the traditional project and lowest in the innovative
project (only 1%). The Scheffé procedure indicated that there was
significantly more isolated behavior in the traditional project than
in the average of the old neighborhood and the innovative project
($F = 6.64$, $df = 2/66$, $p < .05$).

RECLAIMING SOCIAL SPACE

These findings convincingly demonstrate that outdoor public space
is an important medium for social exchange in the low-income
neighborhood. Over three-quarters of outdoor behavior across all
environmental sites was social in nature. Of particular interest is
the role played by "informal" public spaces in supporting the casual
social behavior so typical of the low-income neighborhood. For
example, in the old neighborhood, 90% of outdoor behavior
occurred along the sidewalk, near entranceways, on stoops, and
along the curb. People tended to meet one another while engaged
in different though complementary activities, and used such opportunities for informal and casual social exchange. In addition, the
grassy areas in the traditional project, which designers have
pointed to proudly as evidence of newfound open urban space, were
almost never used because they were fenced off for an aesthetic
rather than a functional impact. The creatively designed adventure
playground in the innovative project was also little used. In fact,
most of the active recreation in both projects was ball playing. The
children we observed clearly preferred open spaces for ball playing
rather than more playground equipment. In the innovative project,
the adventure playground equipment went almost unused, while
children usurped available space for ball playing, including the
observation area around the playground, the main access to the
pedestrian mall, and even the floor of the amphitheater.

USING OUTDOOR SPACE

The total number of subjects observed under the AM procedure in the old neighborhood, the traditional project, and the innovative project was 287, 280, and 178, respectively. An analysis of subjects by age group in the three environmental settings itself reflected an interesting difference between sites. This analysis involved comparing the percent of subjects observed outdoors during this study and the actual percentage of residents in each setting as reflected in the 1970 census. The census data showed that both projects had approximately equal numbers of youths and adults, while the old neighborhood had approximately a 6-to-4 ratio of adults to youths. The observed frequencies closely conformed to the actual frequencies in the old neighborhood and the traditional project. In the innovative project, however, the observed frequencies reflected a stronger preference for using the outdoor environment on the part of youths relative to adults. The difference between observed and expected frequencies of youths and adults in the innovative project was statistically significant by chi-square test ($x^2 = 16.38$, $df = 1$, $p < .001$).

Table 3 shows the percent of subjects in each activity category across the three environmental settings for all subjects and for youths and adults separately. Let us examine first the data for all subjects. In all settings, leisure activity represented approximately 50% of outdoor behavior. Differences between settings occurred in the relative distribution of active recreation and functional behavior. Active recreation was least in the old neighborhood, somewhat higher in the traditional project, and highest in the innovative project. Functional activity showed exactly the opposite pattern. These differences between settings were statistically significant at the .001 level ($\chi^2 = 43.3$, $df = 4$).* For youths the differences between settings were statistically significant ($x^2 = 32.9$, $df = 4$, $p < .001$), while for adults the differences were not significant. The activity distributions for the two age groups

---

*All x^2 tests on the AM data were performed on the actual frequency of subjects in each cell. To facilitate interpretation, the tables reflect the percent of subjects in each cell.

Table 3. Percent of Behavior in Each Activity Category
by Age Group across the Three Environmental Settings

Age group	Behavior category	Environmental setting		
		Old neighborhood	Traditional project	Innovative project
All subjects	Active recreation	6	15	27
	Leisure	53	51	51
	Functional	41	34	22
Youths	Active recreation	11	28	36
	Leisure	39	41	47
	Functional	50	31	17
Adults	Active recreation	4	2	10
	Leisure	60	61	60
	Functional	36	37	30

considered separately were generally similar to that for all subjects.
However, for youths the level of active recreation was relatively
higher and of leisure relatively lower than for adults.

RECLAIMING FUNCTIONAL SPACE

It is interesting to note the relationship of activity level to specific
physical features of the outdoor environment. In the old neighborhood, 90% of outdoor behavior occurred along the sidewalk, much
of it in the vicinity of entrances to residential or commercial
establishments. In both projects, the most used environmental
feature was benches. Surprisingly, in the innovative project the
adventure playground was little used. In the traditional project, as
expected, the large grassy areas were almost totally vacant.

The pattern of bench use in the project environments
reflected clearly the intimate relationship between design and
function. The most used benches in both projects were those along
the major entranceways to the projects, which overlooked both the

safety

streets of the old neighborhood and the entrances to many of the project buildings. This was especially interesting in the innovative project, where benches that afforded good viewing of many people engaged in daily activities were greatly preferred over the more creatively designed benches in the interior of the project. The differential use of the innovative project environment across age groups can also be explained in functional terms. The innovative project proved a remarkably successful social setting for youths but not for adults. Adults were also less inclined than youths to use the outdoor spaces in the innovative project. Although the innovative design met the recreational demands of youths, it did not provide for the many functional needs that attract adults outdoors. The old neighborhood was probably attractive to adults precisely because it met a wide range of functional needs in addition to recreation and leisure.

People gather – laundrymat

SOME IMPLICATIONS FOR URBAN DESIGN

Several propositions concerning the relationship between behavior and urban design emerge from the study's findings. (1) Effective urban design requires evaluation at a functional in addition to an aesthetic level. (2) Public open space provides an important avenue for social contact in the low-income neighborhood. (3) Much of the social function in the low-income neighborhood is played by "informal" social spaces, i.e., spaces designed for one function, which in practice support a range of social activities not anticipated by the original designer. These propositions are consistent with and lend empirical support to the viewpoints concerning design and behavior that have emerged from previous speculations (Fried & Gleicher, 1970; Gans, 1962; Hartman, 1963; Jacobs, 1961) concerning low-income urban neighborhoods.

It appears that the lower level of socializing in the traditional project relative to the older low-income neighborhood was due to two factors. First, the fault seems to lie more in badly designed outdoor space rather than in high-rise living *per se*. The innovatively designed project environment proved more supportive of active socializing between youths than did the environment of the old neighborhood. Second, an aesthetically designed environment without the potential to support a range of functional activities is not sufficient to attract outdoor socializing between adults. A better solution would be a project integrated with the commercial and adult recreational attractions of the old neighborhood. The ideal situation would encourage mixed functional uses — recreational, leisure, consumer, task-oriented — in order to attract individuals to use available open space. Then, innovative design features — nooks, benches, tables — might be added to facilitate and support the informal social contact likely to occur between persons who meet accidentally while pursuing diversified tasks in such multifunctional space.

The study lends some implications concerning the design of "street furniture," such as benches. The effective design of street furniture includes not only its form but also its location relative to other street furniture and to adjacent activity patterns. Unfortunately, the benches along the entranceways of both projects, which were well situated for viewing behavior, were poorly designed as physical props or supports for socializing. Arranged in a straight row, they forced individuals to sit shoulder-to-shoulder, and inhibited rather than supported active social contact. Also, since the benches were situated in the flow of pedestrian traffic, a passerby stopping to talk to a seated person became a hindrance to the free flow of traffic. The design of stoops in the old neighborhood, in contrast, allowed face-to-face conversation, while also permitting an interested passerby to comfortably join the conversation by stepping out of the line of traffic.

SUMMARY

As predicted, the old neighborhood and the innovative project were characterized by higher levels of social behavior than was the traditional project. Interestingly, though, socializing was actually greater in the innovative project than in either of the other sites. This latter finding was due particularly to the successful functioning of the innovative project environment as a recreational space for youths. Concerning the relative frequency of behavior types, the old neighborhood unexpectedly showed the highest level of functional activities relative to recreation and leisure. Apparently, the street life of the old neighborhood was based less on its directly meeting recreational and leisure needs than on its providing opportunities for residents to casually interact while pursuing a range of diverse tasks. Most important was the manner in which these inner-city residents coped with the challenge of an urban environment that was incongruent with the informal nature of social process in the community. Although residents were powerless to physically alter their neighborhood, they demonstrated a remarkably active, energetic, and creative stance in usurping and redefining available space to suit the functional demands of group life.

REFERENCES

Brower, S. *Outdoor recreation as a function of the urban housing environment.* Fifth annual meeting of the Environment Design Research Association, Childhood-City Workshop, Virginia Polytechnic Institute, 1973.

Dotson, F. Patterns of voluntary association among urban working-class families. *American Sociological Review*, 1951, *16*, 687–693.

Fried, M. Grieving for a lost home. In L. G. Duhl (Ed.), *The urban condition: People and policy in the metropolis.* New York: Basic Books, 1963.

Fried, M., & Gleicher, P. Some sources of residential satisfaction in an urban slum. In H. M. Proshansky, W. H. Ittelson, & L. G. Rivlin (Eds.), *Environmental psychology: Man and his physical setting.* New York: Holt, Rinehart & Winston, 1970.

Gans, H. J. *Social and physical planning for the elimination of poverty.* Paper presented at Conference of the American Institute of Planners, Washington, D. C., 1962.

Hartman, C. The limitations of public housing: Relocation choices in a working-class community. *Journal of American Institute of Planners*, 1963, *24*, 283–296.

Hollingshead, A. B., & Rogler, L. H. Attitudes toward slums and public housing in Puerto Rico. In L. J. Duhl (Ed.), *The urban condition: People and policy in the metropolis.* New York: Basic Books, 1963.

Ittelson, W. H., Rivlin, L. G., & Proshansky, H. M. The use of behavioral maps in environmental psychology. In H. M. Proshansky, W. H. Ittelson, & L. G. Rivlin (Eds.), *Environmental psychology: Man and his physical setting.* New York: Holt, Rhinehart & Winston, 1970.

Jacobs, J. *The death and life of great American cities.* New York: Vintage Books, 1961.

Michelson, W. *Man and his urban environment: A sociological approach.* Reading, Massachussetts: Addison-Wesley, 1970.

Newman, O. *Defensible space.* New York: Macmillan, 1972.

Rainwater, L. Fear and the house-as-haven in the lower class. In B. J. Frieden & R. Morris (Eds.), *Urban planning and social policy.* New York: Basic Books, 1968.

Scheffé, H. *The analysis of variance.* New York: Wiley, 1959.

Whyte, W. F. *Street corner society.* Chicago: University of Chicago Press, 1943.

Yancy, W. L. Architecture, interaction and social control. *Environment and Behavior,* 1971, *3* (1), 3–21.

Young, M., & Willmott, P. *Family and kinship in East London.* Baltimore: Pelican Books, 1962.

CHAPTER 3

Social Coping and Environmental Satisfaction in a University Megadorm*

Pressed by the demands of both restricted funds and limited space, university planners have demonstrated an increasing proclivity toward viewing the high-rise megadorm as a ready solution for students' residential housing needs. This decision is particularly disturbing as a number of recent research studies concerned with quality of life in student residential environments have reported reduced satisfaction with the living environment and social atmosphere in high-rise megadorms in contrast to low-rise dormitory settings. Some findings have, for example, pointed to less positive social behavior and group cooperation (Bickman, Teger, Gabriele, McLaughlin, Berger, & Sunaday, 1973) in high- as opposed to low-rise student housing. In addition, crowding in dormitory settings has been shown to relate to increased stress along with decreased social contact (Valins & Baum, 1973), more negative ratings of living space (Eoyang, 1974), and more negative interpersonal attitudes (Baron, Mandel, Adams, & Griffen, 1976).

An extensive investigation of the environmental psychology of high-rise student housing was conducted by Van der Ryn and Silverstein (1967) at the University of California at Berkeley. It involved an effort to explain excessively high vacancy rates in newly constructed high-rise towers by examining the discrepancy

---

*The research discussed in this chapter was conducted in collaboration with Brian L. Wilcox.

between user needs and the existing environmental design. As mentioned earlier, Wheeler (1968) looked into the behavioral consequences of the double-loaded corridor often used in high-rise residence halls. He suggested in his results that the benefits of a different design involving the separation of the two sides of the corridor by a central lounge–study area would eliminate much of the noise heard in such corridors and afford a setting in which students might interact socially on both sides.

A number of authors have, in addition, stressed the impact that the university residential living environment exerts on student development (Chickering, 1972; Feldman & Newcomb, 1969; Newcomb, 1962, 1966). These authors have suggested that the immediate living environment generates a wide-ranging impact on student life in spheres such as intellectual productivity, satisfaction with college life, emotional development, and the maturation of interpersonal relationship skills. Given this, and the fact that for many students the university residence environment represents the dominant locale for their time, energy, and activity, Heilweil (1973) has stressed the need for evaluative research on the psychological impact of the university residential living environment. He adds that the alternative is to relinquish this responsibility to chance, intuition, and custodial rather than functional and psychological concerns.

AN ENVIRONMENTAL SURVEY

The purpose of the present study was to extend this area of investigation to include an analysis of a number of important social psychological processes underlying environmental satisfaction in residential living. Specifically, the study involved (1) a comparison of environmental satisfaction in high- and low-rise dormitory settings, (2) an investigation of a social coping strategy, the formation of proximate friendship networks, utilized by students in adapting to contrasting residential environments, and (3) an analysis of the interaction between social competence and type of environment in affecting both coping style and living satisfaction.

The lack of previous research in this area at a corresponding level of analysis made the testing of specific hypotheses impossible. However, some previous work dealing with the more general issue of interactionism in personality research did offer a useful investigative framework. A number of studies (Bem & Allen, 1974; Ekehammar, 1974; Endler & Hunt, 1966, 1968, 1969; Mischel, 1968, 1969, 1973; Price & Bouffard, 1974; Raush, Dittmann, & Taylor, 1959; Raush, Farbman, & Llewellyn, 1960) concerned with investigating personal versus situational effects in predicting social behavior have found that the interactions between personal and environmental variables account for an especially large proportion of the total behavioral variance. Thus, in approaching the present study, it was anticipated that (1) high-rise dormitories would be characterized by a lower level of living satisfaction than would low-rise dormitories, and (2) the interaction between type of environment and social competence would be of particular importance in predicting both social coping and environmental satisfaction.

Two types of student residential environments were compared in the study: a high-rise megadorm and a number of low-rise dormitories. The megadorm consisted of a tower of 10 floors occupied by males and a tower of 13 floors occupied by females. The megadorm housed approximately 3,000 students. The low-rise dormitories consisted of two dormitories for males (one of 2 floors and one of 4 floors) and two dormitories for females (one of 2 floors and one of 5 floors). Each low-rise dormitory housed approximately 250 students.

SURVEY MEASURES

Social Competence

Social competence was measured by the Texas Social Behavior Inventory (TSBI), developed by Helmreich and his co-workers (Helmreich & Stapp, 1974; Helmreich, Stapp, & Ervin, 1974). The authors report that the TSBI offers a highly reliable instrument for assessing individuals' self-perception of social competence and social self-esteem. They note that the instrument demonstrates a high level of construct validity based on its relationship with other measures of ability, attitude, and personality. For example, the TSBI has been found to correlate highly ($r = .50, p < .001$) with the self-esteem scale of the California Personality Inventory (Gough, 1964). Factor analysis has yielded factors of confidence and dominance along with social competence. Representative items from the 16-item (5-point scale) TSBI are: I feel I can confidently approach and deal with anyone I meet; when I work on a committee I like to take charge of things; I feel confident of my appearance; I have no doubts about my social competence.

Social Coping

Through discussions with dormitory staff, especially student activities coordinators, it was felt that for university freshmen new to the campus setting an important coping strategy involved the establishment of proximal and easily accessible friendship networks. This assumption was reinforced through input from resident assistants that a chief complaint of dissatisfied residents in the megadorm concerned social isolation. Based on this information, we decided to develop a sociometric technique to measure the level of friendship networks established within a proximate relationship to the resident's room. We felt a valid measure should tap meaningful relationships in addition to casual social contacts. Thus, a sociometric index was developed oriented toward measuring friendships at three levels of intimacy: casual–recreational, personal–conversational, and supportive. The items that tapped each of these levels respectively asked the respondent to identify (1) a friend to join you in a casual outing to a film or a sports event, (2) a friend to join you in a personal conversation where attitudes and values are shared, (3) a friend to join you in discussing an intimate personal problem concerning your feelings about a member of your family. In responding to the sociometric measure, students were asked to choose up to five friends at each intimacy level and to identify their location relative to their own room. For quantification purposes, choices were designated as proximate when they were located within a distance of five rooms from the resident's room. All choices within this range were weighted (from 5 for a first choice to 1 for a fifth choice), and a final score was obtained by summing over the three friendship levels.

Environmental Satisfaction

A measure of satisfaction with the living environment was developed, which was composed of 10 scaled (7-point) items. The items measured satisfaction with meeting people and making friends, recreation, opportunities and places for personal conversation, finding help or support for a personal problem, comfort, privacy, student influence in policy decisions, physical layout of building and rooms, furnishings, and overall feeling about living in the particular dormitory. The predictive validity of the satisfaction scale was determined by correlating the satisfaction score with residents' decisions to remain in or leave the particular dormitory for the next academic year. A statistically significant correlation was obtained ($r = .41$, $df = 156$, $p < .01$).

SURVEY ADMINISTRATION

Subjects in the study were 129 second-semester freshmen who were residents of on-campus university housing at a large southwestern university. The sample included 55 males and 74 females, all of whom volunteered for the study. No subjects were accepted from any dormitory areas designated for special programming. Only freshmen were used in order to limit self-selection for specific living arrangements likely to occur for advanced students with prior living experience on campus. Nevertheless, the sample was not random, and in order to examine for any systematic population bias across dormitories, the subject samples from each dormitory were compared along a number of demographic indicators (family economic level, racial distribution, geographic background). There were no significant differences between dormitories on any of these measures.

The personal, social coping, and satisfaction measures were included together in a survey that required approximately 15 minutes for completion. The surveys were handed out to each subject personally by the resident assistant on his or her floor. The student was asked to complete the survey anonymously and to return it to the assistant's mailbox within two days. A cover letter signed by the principal investigator explained that the survey concerned satisfactions and dissatisfactions in dormitory living. The survey was conducted simultaneously across all settings one month before the end of the spring semester. Trained experimental assistants working with the resident assistants assured a standardized administration procedure. Surveys were administered in each dormitory on floors randomly selected from those that met the experimental criteria (i.e., those free of special programming). One hundred and twenty forms were administered in the megadorm, and 60 and 100 forms were administered in the male and female low-rise dorms, respectively. The return rate was 62% in the megadorms and 58% in the low-rise dorms. In order to decrease disproportionality in cell size, 32 subjects were removed in a random manner from three cells with disproportionately high N's.

DISSATISFACTION IN THE MEGADORM

Table 4 shows mean responses by type of dormitory setting and level of social competence on the environmental satisfaction and social coping measures. In the statistical analysis social competence was treated as a blocking variable, with high and low groups established through a median split. Data were analyzed in two-factor analyses of variances (dormitory × social competence) with satisfaction and coping as dependent variables.

Residents of the megadorm scored significantly lower on the measure of environmental satisfaction than did students in the low-rise dormitories ($F = 20.18$, $df = 1/125$, $p < .001$). The range of dissatisfaction in the megadorm was quite broad and included

Table 4. Mean Scores by Dormitory and Competence on
the Environmental Satisfaction and Social Coping
Measures

Measures	Low-rise dormitories		Megadorm	
	High competent	Low competent	High competent	Low competent
Living satisfaction	52.99	45.45	38.05	41.88
Social coping	17.95	16.56	13.73	19.35

feelings about social contact and support, features of the physical environment, and student involvement in policy decisions. These findings are consistent with the negative picture of residential life in high-rise as opposed to low-rise dormitory settings that has emerged from earlier environmental research (Baron *et al.*, 1976; Bickman *et al.*, 1973; Valins & Baum, 1973).

SATISFACTION AND SOCIAL COMPETENCE

On the measure of environmental satisfaction, a significant interaction was found between type of dormitory and level of social competence ($F = 7.60$, $df = 1/125$, $p < .007$). In the low-rise dormitories, high competent residents, as might be anticipated, scored higher on the environmental satisfaction measure than did low competent residents. In the megadorm, however, low competent students were, surprisingly, more satisfied than high competent students. Clearly, the megadorm environment presents a highly unusual and rather complex picture of student satisfaction and dissatisfaction. How might this intially surprising finding of the relationship between satisfaction and competence in the megadorm be explained? The answer will become clear as we turn to an examination of the important role of social coping strategies in the context of student residential life.

COPING AND SOCIAL COMPETENCE

On the coping measure, a significant interaction once again emerged between type of dormitory and level of social competence ($F = 4.71$, $df = 1/125$, $p < .03$). This interaction reflected a positive relationship between social competence and coping in the low-rise dormitories, but an inverse relationship between competence and coping in the megadorm. This interaction indicates that different kinds of coping occurred in the contrasting types of environmental settings. In the satisfying low-rise dormitories, more socially competent students were more effective than less competent ones in developing proximate friendship networks. In the dissatisfying megadorm, in contrast, it appears that socially competent students chose not to establish such friendships, in effect permitting less competent students to develop networks of their own. There are some data to support this interpretation. Although the effect was not statistically significant, a strong tendency emerged for high competent megadorm residents to form more friendships outside of the megadorm than did low competent residents.

COPING AND SATISFACTION

If the nature of social coping in residential life is to offer an explanation of the relationship between satisfaction and social competence, it is imperative to demonstrate a relationship between coping strategy and level of environmental satisfaction. The relationship of coping to satisfaction was examined in a simple analysis of variance design, with coping as the independent variable (high and low coping groups were formed through a median split) and satisfaction as the dependent variable. A significant F was found at the .001 level ($F = 12.18$, $df = 1/127$), with residents in the high coping group more satisfied than those in the low coping group. Thus, the role of social coping in residential life provides an interpretation of the surprising inverse relationship between competence and satisfaction in the megadorm. As more socially competent students in the megadorm chose not to develop friendship networks, less competent students were able to establish friendships of their own, and these dormitory-based friendships exerted a strong positive influence on overall satisfaction with residential life. The important interactions between type of environment and social competence in affecting both coping and satisfaction found in the present study are consistent with a growing body of social psychological research that has emphasized an interactional framework in predicting social behavior (Ekehammar, 1974; Endler & Hunt, 1966, 1968, 1969; Mischel, 1968, 1969, 1973; Price & Bouffard, 1973; Raush et al., 1959, 1960).

APPLYING THE SURVEY FINDINGS

These findings from the evaluation survey were used as feedback to relevant campus administrators for deciding on policy or design alternatives, and as a baseline against which to measure the impact of any changes based on the feedback. Feedback sessions were held with staff in the megadorm environment, including the dormitory director, assistant director, and student life coordinators. Sessions were conducted in a collaborative rather than expert fashion. First, findings from the study were presented and discussed. This was followed by a brainstorming session oriented toward generating a range of solution alternatives. Finally, possible solutions were reconsidered in the light of administrative priorities, financial constraints, likely success, and the time period necessary for implementation. The solutions that emerged from this process were then accepted as workable strategies for improving student satisfaction, which could be implemented over a relatively short-term period.

The particular change strategies that were developed were of two types: (1) administrative policy revisions oriented toward facilitating students' adaptive coping efforts with existing environmental realities, and (2) decisions concerning strategic physical remodeling in areas where minimal financial input might generate optimal behavioral benefits. Policy revisions included: resident assistant training programs based on the study's findings, a special orientation program to the megadorm environment, an emphasis on increased social contact between students and residence hall staff at all levels, increased social functions at the floor level to facilitate the establishment of friendship networks, and greater administrative responsiveness to students' requests for specific roommate changes. Physical design changes included construction of partitions in the huge dining area to facilitate group contact and social interaction, and refurnishing of the badly deteriorated lounge areas on each floor to encourage social participation and group formation.

SUMMARY

These results support the negative picture of residential life in high-rise as opposed to low-rise dormitory settings reported in earlier research (Baron et al., 1976; Bickman et al., 1973; Valins & Baum, 1973). Residents of the megadorm were significantly less satisfied than residents of the low-rise dormitories, with the range of dissatisfaction quite broad, including attitudes toward the social environment, physical setting, and administrative atmosphere. Especially interesting was the important role of social coping in residential life. In fact, the positive relationship between coping and environmental satisfaction provided an explanation of the intially surprising finding that social competence and satisfaction were inversely related in the megadorm. It appears that as more socially competent residents chose to establish friendships outside of the megadorm, less socially competent students were able to develop dormitory-based friendships of their own, and these social contacts related strongly to overall living satisfaction in the residential context. We should, of course, exercise some caution in generalizing the present findings to students in other university settings. The subject sample we have examined here was select both in terms of the characteristics of students who initially chose dormitory living at this university and in terms of those residents who elected to respond to the survey. A complete model of coping in residential living environments will have to await further investigation in other campus settings, involving a broad sampling of student values, social styles, and educational orientation.

REFERENCES

Baron, R. M., Mandel, D. R., Adams, C. A., & Griffen, L. M. Effects of social density in university residential environments. *Journal of Personality and Social Psychology*, 1976, 34, 434–466.

Bem, D. J., & Allen, A. On predicting some of the people some of the time: The search for cross-situational consistencies in behavior. *Psychological Review*, 1974, 81, 506–520.

Bickman, L., Teger, A., Gabriele, T., McLaughlin, C., Berger, M., & Sunaday, E., Dormitory density and helping behavior. *Environment and Behavior*, 1973, 5, 465–490.

Chickering, A. W. *Education and identity*. San Francisco: Jossey-Bass, 1972.

Ekehammar, B. Interactionism in personality from a historical perspective. *Psychological Bulletin*, 1974, 81, 1026–1048.

Endler, N. S., & Hunt, J. McV. Sources of behavioral variance as measured by the S-R inventory of anxiousness. *Psychological Bulletin*, 1966, 65, 336–346.

Endler, N. S., & Hunt, J. McV. S-R inventories of hostility and comparisons of the proportions of variance from persons, responses and situations for hostility and anxiousness. *Journal of Personality and Social Psychology*, 1968, 9, 114–123.

Endler, N. S., & Hunt, J. McV. Generalizability of contributions from sources of variance in the S-R inventories of anxiousness. *Journal of Personality*, 1969, 37, 1–24.

Eoyang, C. K. Effects of group size and privacy in residential crowding. *Journal of Personality and Social Psychology*, 1974, 30, 389–392.

Feldman, K., & Newcomb, T. M. *The impact of college on students Vols. 1 & 2*. San Francisco: Jossey-Bass, 1969.

Gough, H. G. *California Personality Inventory: Manual*. Palo Alto: Consulting Psychologists' Press, 1964.

Heilweil, M. The influence of dormitory architecture on resident behavior. *Environment and Behavior*, 1973, 5, 377–412.

Helmreich, R., & Stapp, J. Short forms of the Texas Social Behavior Inventory (TSBI), an objective measure of self-esteem. *Bulletin of the Psychonomic Society*, 1974, 4(5a), 473–475.

Helmreich, R., Stapp, J., & Ervin, C. The Texas Social Behavior Inventory (TSBI): An objective measure of self-esteem or social competence. *Journal Supplement Abstract Service Catalog of Selected Documents in Psychology*, 1974.

Mischel, W. *Personality and assessment.* New York: Wiley, 1968.

Mischel, W. Continuity and change in personality. *American Psychologist,* 1969, *24,* 1012–1018.

Mischel, W. Toward a cognitive social learning reconceptualization of personality. *Psychological Review,* 1973, *80,* 252–283.

Newcomb, T. M. Student peer-group influence and intellectual outcomes of college experience. In R. Sutherland, W. Holtzman, E. Koile, & B. Smith (Eds.), *Personality factors on campus.* Austin, Texas: Hogg Foundation for Mental Health, 1962.

Newcomb, T. M. Research on student characteristics: Current approaches. In L. Dennis & J. Kauffman (Eds.), *The college and the students.* Washington, D. C.: American Council on Education, 1966.

Price, R. H., & Bouffard, D. L. Behavioral appropriateness and situational constraint and dimensions of social behavior. *Journal of Personality and Social Psychology,* 1974, *30,* 579–586.

Raush, H. L., Dittman, A. T., & Taylor, T. J. Person, setting and change in social interaction. *Human Relations,* 1959, *12,* 361–379.

Raush, H. L., Farbman, I., & Llewellyn, L. G. Person, setting and change in social interaction: II. A normal control study. *Human Relations,* 1960, *13,* 305–333.

Valins, S., & Baum, A. Residential group size, social interaction, and crowding. *Environment and Behavior,* 1973, *5,* 421–439.

Van der Ryn, S. & Silverstein, M. *Dorms at Berkeley: An environmental analysis.* New York: Educational Facilities Laboratories, 1967.

Wheeler, L. *Behavioral research for architectural planning and design.* Terre Haute, Indiana: Ewing Miller Associates, 1968.

CHAPTER 4

Coping with Environmental Change: A Social Systems Model

Change in the physical environment affords an especially interesting context within which to examine the process of environmental coping. Recent work conducted by the Environmental Psychology Program at the City University of New York* in the psychiatric pavilion of a large municipal hospital, which we will call Bridgehaven, provided a unique opportunity for investigating how people cope with environmental change. In order to test the behavioral effects of variation in ward physical environment, we received permission to plan, finance, and direct the extensive remodeling of an admission ward in the hospital. This chapter discusses the fascinating manner in which ward staff members dealt with the challenge presented by this large-scale change in the ward setting.

A small body of research has accumulated, which has investigated the relationship between physical milieu and patient behavior in psychiatric treatment settings. Ittelson, Proshansky, and Rivlin, (1970b), for example, compared various psychiatric hospitals and found that behavioral options differed dramatically over types of hospitals. In both a city and a state hospital, patients exhibited significantly more passive, withdrawn behavior than in a

---

*The ward remodeling was supported by a grant from the National Institute of Mental Health to William Ittelson. The initial planning of the remodeling changes was coordinated by William Ittelson and Susan Saegert.

private hospital, though, of course, physical environment was but
one factor that distinguished the hospitals in their study. Design
variations within hospitals have also been shown to affect patient
behavior. Ittelson, Proshansky, and Rivlin, (1970a) reported more
social interaction and more active isolated behavior in single-
patient rooms than in two-, three-, or four-patient rooms. Sommer
and Ross (1958) succeeded in doubling social interaction between
patients on a geriatric ward by rearranging the furniture in the dayroom. The purpose of the present study was to extend this area of
investigation by examining the behavioral consequences of the
planned remodeling on a large scale of an existing psychiatric ward.

WARD REMODELING

The remodeling was based on the preferences and dissatisfactions
expressed by patients and staff at Bridgehaven, and on our
observations of behavior on the ward. The design was intended to
encourage successful social interaction and to discourage withdrawal. Before remodeling, the walls on the ward were dirty and
peeling and were marred by scribbling that was rarely cleaned.
Furniture on the ward was old, worn, and rather uncomfortable.
The remodeling was designed to improve qualitatively the ward
atmosphere and to achieve a number of specific behavioral effects.
The changes concerned with improving ward atmosphere included
repainting the ward and the addition of new furniture. A range of
bright colors was chosen for the repainting, and attractive, modern
furniture was added in the dayrooms and bedrooms. A number of
additional changes on the ward were concerned with creating areas
on the ward that afforded a range of social options — from a high
degree of privacy to a high level of social participation. A private
sector was created in the bedrooms by installing six-foot-high
partitions, creating a number of two-bed sections in each
dormitory. A table and two comfortable chairs were installed in a
screened-off area of each bedroom to allow for private
conversations. Small group interaction was encouraged in one day-

room where new tables and chairs were arranged in small social groupings. Larger group socializing could occur at large tables in the dining room.

EVALUATING THE EFFECTS OF CHANGE

There was an opportunity to employ an experimental control at Bridgehaven since a second admissions ward was available that was identical to the remodeled ward before change. The Posttest Only Control Design (Campbell & Stanley, 1963) was used; random assignment of subjects to experimental conditions was assured by a computerized randomization procedure already operational in the hospital. Observations of patient behavior on the two wards were conducted using the behavioral mapping procedure developed by Ittelson, Rivlin, and Proshansky (1970) and extended by Holahan (1972). Twenty-five patients were randomly selected for observation on each of the two wards. Experimental measures were initiated six months after the remodeling was completed to allow sufficient time for enduring ward routines to become established, and were collected in an identical manner on the two wards during a simultaneous five-week period. Five patients were studied per week on each ward. Observation sessions of 75 minutes were conducted on both the morning and afternoon of Mondays and Thursdays. A time-sampling procedure was used in which an instantaneous recording of each patient's behavior was performed at five-minute intervals. There were 15 intervals per observation session, resulting in a total of 60 observations per patient over four sessions.

The observations on which the social systems analysis is based consisted of a detailed record kept by the principal experimenter of events on the ward throughout the planning, remodeling, and post-change periods. The following three categories of observations were recorded:

1. Formal and informal interactions between CUNY investigators and ward staff, e.g., cooperative planning sessions for

design decisions, casual sharing of personal reactions to the environmental changes.

2. Daily ward routines: (a) Process and content of ward staff meetings; (b) role behavior of different staff groups, e.g., habitual ward duties carried out by each group, typical interpersonal contacts between staff groups; (c) unobtrusive measures, e.g., personalization of space, arrangement of new furniture by ward staff, occurrence and repair of damage to the new environment.

3. Critical incidents, e.g., staff resistance to an environmental change, a flare-up between staff members.

INCREASED SOCIAL ACTIVITY

We predicted that after the remodeling, patients on the remodeled ward would engage in more social behavior and be less passive and withdrawn than patients on the unchanged control ward. These hypotheses were supported. Table 5 depicts mean behavior per subject in each behavior category on the remodeled and control wards. The mean difference between the two wards in total social interaction was statistically significant at the .05 level with a directional test ($t = 1.78$, $df = 40$). The mean difference between the two wards in total isolated behavior was statistically significant at the .05 level with a directional test ($t = 1.84$, $df = 40$).

A SOCIAL SYSTEMS MODEL OF COPING

The initial task of presenting the behavioral data from the study has been done elsewhere (Holahan & Saegert, 1973). That paper was restricted in focus to view behavioral change as a *direct* function of change in the immediate physical context. While such an approach was useful for communicating initial findings demonstrating the relationship between ward design and behavior, we have become increasingly impressed with the need for a more complete analysis, incorporating the range of psychological, social, and administrative repercussions that mediated the behavioral

Table 5. Patient Behavior on the Remodeled and
Control Wards

Behavior categories	Remodeled ward		Control ward	
	$\overline{X}$	SD	$\overline{X}$	SD
Social				
Social with patients	7.3	6.99	5.1	6.00
Social with staff	3.8	1.28	2.6	2.88
Social with visitors	3.2	4.96	1.1	3.60
Total social	14.3	11.56	8.8	7.50
Nonsocial				
Engaged in activity	9.5	7.44	9.9	6.74
Observing activity	5.6	9.24	3.5	3.39
Walking	6.7	6.63	8.3	6.97
Total nonsocial active	21.8	14.54	21.7	9.22
Isolated passive awake	7.1	5.47	11.5	7.51
Isolated passive sleeping	11.8	13.65	15.8	14.93
Total isolated passive	18.9	14.91	27.3	14.33

effects. The purpose of this chapter is to present such an analysis by (a) discussing important changes in the social system of the ward that were caused by the physical changes and in part mediated the effects on patient behavior, and (b) describing a time-ordered process in which to understand and anticipate such social system changes.

Environmental research in psychiatric settings has typically focused almost exclusively on the behavior of individual patients. The following analysis, in contrast, consists of an effort to conceptualize the ward as a social system, with a particular emphasis on the network of interlocking behaviors of ward staff members. Such change in staff behavior warrants complete analysis both because it represents a significant level of the change process in its own right and because in part it functioned as a mediating link in the process whereby environmental change altered patient behavior. Specifically, we will analyze a range of surprising and significant changes in the role behavior of ward staff which unfolded during the environmental change period. We have conceptualized these role changes as part of a more general environmental change process involving four distinct temporal phases — petrification, unfreezing, resistance, and personalization.

PETRIFICATION

One of the most compelling phenomena we observed on first entering Bridgehaven was a "petrification" of the ward environment. Over time, the established structure of the physical environment had become rigidly set, with both staff and patients viewing these established patterns as practically unalterable. This petrification pervaded the entire physical environment, including standard ward design, the usual types and arrangements of furnishings, and typical color preferences. Sommer and Ross (1958) have referred to this phenomenon as "institutional sanctity." In fact, however, such petrification extends far beyond an inflexibility in physical setting and pervades the character of the entire institution, including standard ward routines and behavioral norms (cf. Goffman, 1961). We were especially impressed by the extent to which rigidity and inflexibility had colored the nature of staff role behavior on the ward. Before the environmental changes, role behaviors on the ward were rigidly defined, affording little role latitude or flexibility for individual interpretation of role obligations. In addition, role relationships were strictly hierarchical, with implicit norms severely restricting both feedback and the exertion of social power from lower to upper staff echelons.

The role of physician on the ward was characterized by unquestioned authority and limited contact with either patients or other staff. The dominant role behaviors for physicians involved cursory interviews with newly admitted patients and brief notes in the ward journal. The basic strategy for the physician role seemed to be maintaining interpersonal distance in order to assure status security. The role of nurse on the ward involved constant contact with patients, visitors, and nurses' aides. Ward nurses were the real authorities behind the everyday functioning of the ward and were typically overworked and mildly cynical about lasting improvement on the ward. The basic strategy for the nurse role seemed oriented toward efficiently meeting the pragmatic demands of ward life. The role of nurse's aide on the ward involved hard and dirty work in meeting patients' numerous daily needs. The aides were the workhorses on the ward. This group, which was evenly divided between males and females, was typically nonwhite in contrast to both physicians and nurses, who tended to be white. The aides were highly cynical of real change on the ward, tended to be clannish, and evidenced a strategy oriented toward getting their work done and going home. The aide role involved almost no status, and despite aides' greater familiarity with patients, their advice was rarely sought by physicians or nurses.

UNFREEZING

Kurt Lewin (1947) wrote that in order for permanent change to be achieved, the change agent must first unfreeze the old level of performance. In the remodeling study, we realized that productive environmental change would be possible only after the prevailing philosophy of nonchange had been altered. This involved replacing the existing body of expectations that militated against change in the ward system with new expectations that viewed change as both possible and desirable. Lippitt, Watson, and Westley (1958) propose the following factors as essential in the unfreezing process: (a) individuals in the setting must be aware of existing problems, and (b) they must have confidence in the possibility of a more desirable state of affairs.

At Bridgehaven, both of these factors were of importance. Ward staff did not at first consider the lethargic behavioral style on the ward as a therapeutic problem. Also, after having experienced repeated frustrations in initiating change through the hospital bureaucracy, staff evidenced only minimal faith in the prospect of real change. We thus accepted as our first task instilling problem awareness among ward staff. To this end we used data from a pilot behavioral mapping as feedback demonstrating the markedly passive and unsocial quality of daily life on the ward. Since these data clashed sharply with the staff's expectation that the ward should provide an acceptable social atmosphere for patients, it helped to achieve problem awareness, along with a desire for improvement. Our second challenge was to establish confidence in the possibility of change. For this purpose we used an initial change — delivering new equipment to the game room — which was easily effected, highly visible, and likely to produce immediate behavioral effects.

After these initial efforts, we were able to proceed with a cooperative planning effort, which involved agreeing on specific remodeling features and selecting appropriate contractors. This does not convey that unfreezing was completed through our initial strategy. Despite the fact that CUNY funds were available to execute the changes, we worked throughout the planning period against recurring pessimism, bureaucratic entanglements, embedded competitiveness between staff groups, and a diffusion of decision-making responsibility in the hospital. During this period, we played a facilitative role with ward staff, sharing encouragement and listening openly to fears and grievances. Though we operated within the established power structure in the hospital, we made a concerted effort to keep all levels of staff interested and involved in all phases of planning.

RESISTANCE

Some resistance to the changes on the part of ward staff operated covertly even during the prechange period; however, clear resistance surfaced only as real change began and the full implications of change were suddenly felt or imagined. The period during the actual renovation of the admitting ward was not the emotionally positive phase we anticipated and was marked instead by a clear tension and hostility toward us on the part of ward staff. We were especially impressed by how much change was feared and how unwilling staff members were to take personal responsibility for change. Resistance was particularly evident when obvious role changes were involved, as when an environmental change clearly implied a new staff behavior toward patients. Both the administrative structure and peer pressure militated against innovation on the part of staff members. For example, when the ward activity therapist proposed a new treatment philosophy during the change period, he was reprimanded by a supervisor for "overstepping his bounds." Simply initiating environmental change on the ward was not enough, since the impact of change could be undone behaviorally, administratively, or politically. Katz and Kahn (1966) discuss this phenomenon more generally, noting that systems attempt to preserve their character through a quasi-stationary equilibrium, where a movement in one direction is countered by an approximate adjustment in the opposite direction.

A clear example of resistance developed around our effort to install partitions in the large dormitories to create a more private atmosphere for patients in the bedrooms. Although all parties had agreed to the plan in advance, the nursing staff abruptly decided against it on the day carpenters arrived to implement the changes. The staff complained that partitions would make it impossible to survey the bedrooms from the hall as was previously possible. They harassed the unwitting carpenters to such an extent that they quit the job and refused to return until we contacted them directly. A compromise was reached by lowering a number of smaller partitions to facilitate surveillance. However, we later discovered that for two weeks after the changes the evening staff had not assigned any patients to the new bedrooms, choosing instead to put patients in alcoves and in the hallway!

PERSONALIZATION

In retrospect, it appears that resistance to the environmental changes was inversely related to the degree of perceived control staff members felt in producing changes. Resistance decreased dramatically when the ward staff were able to increase their feeling of control over the remodeling by "personalizing" the changes in their surroundings. For example, an open-house party on the newly

completed ward was initiated and organized by ward staff themselves and served as a clear public notice that the changes were their
changes. Also, staff extended the planned changes by adding
touches of their own, as when the nursing assistants made curtains
for the dayroom and dining room with money they raised on the
ward. An interesting aspect of personalization was also observed in
the behavior of patients on the postchange ward. Whereas before
renovation no personalization of space by patients occurred on the
ward, after the change personal articles, such as books, magazines,
towels, powder, and flowers, were observed on the window ledges
of the newly partitioned bedrooms. To some extent we facilitated
this personalization process by encouraging participation in design
decisions across all levels of staff, though much of this
phenomenon operated outside of our control and beyond our
expectations.

Interestingly, openness to change at one level provided an
impetus for a simultaneous openness to change at other levels. As
the remodeling was being completed, ward staff began meeting on
their own initiative to discuss for the first time the development of
a ward treatment philosophy. These meetings offered, in addition,
an opportunity for the open expression of longstanding resent-
ments between different levels of staff. For example, one aide
confronted the physician who headed her staff "team" and
demanded to know if he even knew the names of the aides who
were on his team. He did not. As a result of these meetings, staff
members began to perceive the previously ignored needs, concerns,
and frustrations of members of other staff groups.

During the six months following environmental change, we
observed marked changes in the role behaviors of ward staff. The
previously tight hierarchical structure characterizing role relationships and the use of authority on the ward was considerably relaxed.
Direct and open communication between different level staff
groups was enhanced and included implicit permission for open
negative feedback from lower- to upper-echelon groups. In
addition, roles for the various staff groups demonstrated greater
role latitude, permitting individuals to interpret role obligations on
the basis of their personal level of competence, interest, and skill.

Ward physicians became more open to feedback from other staff members and better in touch with staff and patient needs. Nurses' aides gained the right to contribute suggestions to therapeutic planning, and to express openly negative feedback toward other staff members at all levels. The nurse role, however, changed little during this period, with nurses remaining overworked and somewhat more task-oriented than treatment-oriented.

ENVIRONMENTAL COMPETENCE

It is important to consider the psychological processes involved in translating change in the physical environment at Bridgehaven into change at the level of the ward social system. Two factors appear to be of significance. First, new *expectations* were developed by the physical changes. The improved physical environment implied a greater interest, hope, and involvement in a therapeutic philosophy. Thus, ward staff felt expected to play a stronger role in therapeutic planning and programming. The feeling of increased self-importance ward staff perceived as a result of the environmental improvements was significant in this process. Second, the remodeling task itself demanded a new level of *competence* on the part of ward staff at all levels. Ward staff were forced to demonstrate and practice a range of highly competent behaviors in planning for the changes, from selecting color preferences to determining an optimum number of beds for the new bedrooms. Competence was also demanded from ward staff in executing the changes, from arranging new furniture in the dayroom to keeping painters and patients from interfering in one another's activities. We encouraged this process across all levels of staff by soliciting, facilitating, and legitimizing input from all staff groups throughout the change process.

The increased feeling of competence and effectance on the part of ward staff learned in the environmental change process generalized naturally to other role behaviors involving therapeutic planning, interpersonal staff relations, and more healthy contacts with patients. The enhanced therapeutic atmosphere on the ward

after the remodeling can be explained in terms of the more
competent role behavior of ward staff rather than as a result of a
more positive attitude toward patients. From the beginning ward
staff perceived the remodeling in terms of personal comfort and
ego enhancement rather than as an effort to create a better atmosphere for patients. In fact, one impact of the remodeling was to
accelerate staff expectations for career advancement. For example,
on the postchange ward, one nurse sought an administrative
position, an activity therapist decided to earn a graduate degree,
and an aide planned to enter nursing school. Even the ward janitors
became so involved in the new ward's upkeep that their work was
held up as a model in the hospital's housekeeping unit.

This focus on competence in role behavior helps to explain the
differential impact of the remodeling on the three major staff
groups at Bridgehaven. The remodeling stimulated an increased
ego-involvement in staff roles, and therefore a desire to minimize
any discrepancy between personal competence and actual effectiveness in ward functioning. Before environmental change, the
greatest levels of discrepancy between competence and effectiveness occurred for physicians and aides. In the case of physicians,
this discrepancy was caused because their general withdrawal from
interpersonal contact eliminated the opportunity for application of
their expert training. For aides, the discrepancy was based on their
low status, which did not permit their input in ward decision-
making despite their intimate knowledge of ward functioning at a
pragmatic level. Postremodeling, the discrepancy between
competence and effectiveness was greatly reduced for both groups,
with physicians increasing interpersonal contacts and aides
achieving a somewhat higher status. In the case of nurses, no
discrepancy between competence and effectiveness existed either
before or after the changes since they had both a high level of interpersonal contact and high status in the actual operation of ward
affairs.

REINTERPRETING RESISTANCE

The systematic shift from resistance to personalization discussed
here bears an important similarity to current views of

organizational change. The traditional organizational change model accepted the point of view of the change agent as rational and assumed the resister's view to be irrational. A more current view enhances the role of the resister as vital to the system's survival and underscores the value of the change agent's making positive use of this energy during the change process (Klein, 1969). Our discussion of resistance has stressed our original egocentric view as frustrated change agents. The personalization process represented the involvement in the change process of positive adaptive capacities within the system, which we were forced to respond to and to make use of. The similarity between the personalization of the change process at Bridgehaven and current views of organizational change is especially evident in Watson's (1969) summary of the causes of organizational resistance. He states that resistance will decrease when participants (1) feel that the project is their own, (2) that their autonomy is not threatened, and (3) that the project is kept open to revision on the basis of experience.

SUMMARY

The extensive physical remodeling of a psychiatric admissions ward was conducted to investigate the relationship between ward design and patient behavior. Research in environmental psychology has typically analyzed the effects of physical settings on the behavior of individuals in those settings. We have proposed extending the scope of investigation to include an analysis of how people cope with environmental change, through focusing on changes in the character of the social system in the setting as a key link in the chain of events spurred by environmental change. This chapter presents an analysis of important changes in the ward social system, including staff role relationships, distribution of power, and communication styles, which were generated by the physical changes and mediated the effects on patient behavior. The social system impacts are conceptualized as operating through a time-ordered process of environmental coping involving four phases — petrification, unfreezing, resistance, and personalization.

REFERENCES

Barker, R. G. Explorations in ecological psychology. *American Psychologist*, 1965, *20*, 1–14.

Campbell, D. T., & Stanley, J. C. *Experimental and quasi-experimental design for research*. Chicago: Rand McNally, 1963.

Goffman, E. *Asylums: Essays on the social situation of mental patients and other inmates*. Garden City, N.Y.: Anchor, 1961.

Holahan, C. Seating patterns and patient behavior in an experimental dayroom. *Journal of Abnormal Psychology*, 1972, *80*, 115–124.

Holahan, C., & Saegert, S. Behavioral and attitudinal effects of large-scale variation in the physical environment of psychiatric wards. *Journal of Abnormal Psychology*, 1973, *82*, 454–462.

Ittelson, W. H., Proshansky, H. M., & Rivlin, L. G. Bedroom size and social interaction of the psychiatric ward. *Environment and Behavior*, 1970, *2*, 255–270. (a)

Ittelson, W. H., Proshansky, H. M., & Rivlin, L. G. The environmental psychology of the psychiatric ward. In H. M. Proshansky, W. H. Itelson, & L. G. Rivlin (Eds.), *Environmental psychology: Man and his physical setting*. New York: Holt, Rinehart & Winston, 1970. (b)

Ittelson, W. H., Rivlin, L. G., & Proshansky, H. M. The use of behavioral maps in environmental psychology. In H. M. Proshansky, W. H. Ittelson, & L. G. Rivlin (Eds.), *Environmental psychology: Man and his physical setting*. New York: Holt, Rhinehart & Winston, 1970.

Katz, D. & Kahn, R. L. *The social psychology of organizations*. New York: Wiley, 1966.

Klein, D. Some notes on the dynamics of resistance to change: The defender role. In W. G. Bennis, K. D. Benne, & R. Chin (Eds.), *The planning of change*. New York: Holt, Rinehart & Winston, 1969.

Lewin, K. Frontiers in group dynamics. *Human Relations*, 1947, *1*, 5–41.

Lippitt, R., Watson, J., & Westley, B. *The dynamics of planned change: A comparative study of principles and techniques*. New York: Harcourt, Brace and World, 1958.

Proshansky, H. M., Ittelson, W. H., & Rivlin, L. G. Introduction. In H. M. Proshansky, W. H. Ittelson, & L. G. Rivlin (Eds.), *Environmental psychology: Man and his physical setting*. New York: Holt, Rinehart & Winston, 1970.

Sanoff, H., & Cohn, S. Preface. In H. Sanoff & S. Cohn (Eds.), *Proceedings of the first annual environmental design research association conference*. Raleigh: North Carolina State University, 1970.

Sommer, R., & Ross, H. Social interaction on a geriatrics ward. *International Journal of Social Psychiatry*, 1958, *4*, 128–133.

Watson, G. Resistance to change. In W. G. Bennis, K. D. Benne, & R. Chin (Eds.), *The planning of change*. New York: Holt, Rinehart & Winston, 1969.

PART II

SOCIAL ACCOMMODATION

SOCIAL ACCOMMODATION

In environmental coping we have observed the triumph of
human perseverance in the face of environmental threat.
Occasionally, however, the outcome of the environment–behavior
equation is less salutary. For there are environments that are so
badly designed at the scale of human needs that even the most
vigorous environmental coping cannot wholly reverse their
adverse social consequences. Although this process is less dramatic
than environmental coping, its disturbing human consequences,
though subtle, are substantial and pervasive. For example, in a
poorly designed and socially threatening housing project,
sociologists found that residents, who were normally helpful and cooperative, were unwilling to offer a helping hand even to their
immediate neighbors. In a large municipal psychiatric hospital, I
recall coming across a patient lying alone on a back ward. He told
me that since being brought to the hospital after a suicide attempt,
he had been lying awake for two days, without human contact,
afraid either to leave his bed or to relinquish his vigilant wake-
fulness.

To the extent that environmental coping represents an assimi-
lating of environmental reality to human need, the process we will
consider in this section reflects an *accommodation* of social concern
to environmental restraint. Psychic and occasionally even physical
survival in some environmental settings necessitates that
individuals restrict their interpersonal openness and sensitivity to
accommodate the realistic constraints within which they live. In a

*Doris
Lessing*

violent urban neighborhood, personal safety may compel residents to become less socially cooperative and interpersonally helpful. Sanity in a psychically cacophonous institutional environment may demand accepting a marked degree of interpersonal isolation as an unavoidable feature of daily life. In this section we will examine in detail the process of social accommodation, in which environmental users yield an element of their social life to the harsh realities of socially devastating environmental contexts.

At this point, you may be wondering how social accommodation can possibly reflect a *dy.iamic* process. In fact, the most compelling aspect of observing social accommodation is a realization that even in succumbing to environmental constraints, the inherently dynamic character of human responses to the environment remains evident. When I initiated my research in the settings discussed here, I anticipated finding interpersonal withdrawal occurring in a passive, predictable fashion. I discovered, instead, that even in the breakdown of social bonds, the human processes involved are complex and quite often surprising. In effect, we are less concerned that social deterioration occurs than in observing precisely *how* it comes about. We will see that even when social erosion is unavoidable, human beings reserve some degree of active control, perhaps even dignity, in yielding to the pressure of environmental circumstance.

EXPERIMENTAL INVESTIGATIONS

To investigate how physical environmental leads to the erosion of social bonds, we again sought out those settings that initial research had identified as particularly bankrupt in their functioning as social settings — a psychiatric ward, a poorly designed university setting, a threatening urban setting. While our research agenda in Part I concerned documenting at a holistic and naturalistic level the character of social life in such settings, our investigative concerns here will be more precisely focused on specific environmental features in each setting and on their impacts on specifically defined psychological processes. In the psychiatric ward, we will examine the effects of proxemic design (the pattern of ward seating arrangements) on patients' microinterpersonal behavior. Our concern in the university setting will be the effect of an invasion of privacy on self-disclosure in a counseling setting. In the urban environment, we will investigate the relationship between particular features of the city and altruistic behavior.

The three research studies discussed in this section have again been selected to reflect considerable diversity in terms of the environmental settings investigated and the research methodologies employed. The research designs presented offer three quite different ways to achieve a similar investigative goal — an optimum balance between experimental control and ecological relevance. Because this concern is basic to research in environmental psychology and because the design solutions presented here are somewhat innovative, it will be useful to take a moment to discuss how and why these research strategies developed.

Experimental control will be sought in order to achieve a considerable degree of analytical precision in answering our research questions, precisely defining antecedent conditions (environmental independent variables) while simultaneously restricting extraneous "noise" (unwanted influences from alternative environmental or situational events). A high level of ecological relevance will be maintained in order to learn about human responses as they occur naturalistically, with minimal artificiality introduced through contrived experimental regimentation. Because solutions to these two concerns tend to militate against one another, we will seek flexible design alternatives uniquely congruent with the environmental realities, subject sample characteristics, and specific investigative concerns of each research endeavor. The research strategies in this section will include a laboratory erected in the natural environment, a laboratory analogue of a naturalistic event, and a paper-and-pencil index of help-giving in the city. We feel flexible design solutions like these are essential to environmental psychology, permitting both sufficient precision for decision-making and adequate breadth for policy relevance.

Chapter 5 examines social accommodation in a psychiatric hospital setting where poorly arranged seating patterns on the ward stifle meaningful social participation. By developing an experimental dayroom in the hospital setting, the study is able to examine the effect of systematic variations in ward seating on both the level and quality of interpersonal contact. To gather a rich portrait of socializing in the experimental setting, the study employs a diversified battery of experimental measures, including behavioral mapping, self-report indices, unobtrusive measures, and anecdotal records. We will find that the standard seating arrangements employed in psychiatric settings dramatically reduce the overall amount of social participation on the ward. Even more interesting, in such settings, the quality and intimacy of inter-personal contact is also subtly affected. When patients interact in a poorly designed hospital environment, their contact is less spontaneous, less close, and less warm than in a well-designed social setting. Fascinatingly, the patients themselves are unaware of this social accommodation process.

In Chapter 6, social accommodation is viewed in a university counseling setting where poorly designed space permits an invasion of the counselee's privacy. In this case, our investigation will be conducted using a laboratory analogue design, permitting an analysis of the effect of a controlled invasion of privacy on the level of a counselee's self-disclosure to an interviewer. The design also allows a behavioral index of self-disclosure through tape-recording the interviews, along with self-report measures. We will discover that the process of adjusting to the spatial constraints is again both subtle and surprising. While counselees are as verbally responsive in nonprivate as in private circumstances, when their privacy is invaded, their conversation is less personally "immediate." That is, the respondents begin to discuss the experiences of third parties or people in general rather than their own personal experiences. Again there are discrepancies between these behavioral accommo-dations and counselees' verbal reports about the settings.

Chapter 7 focuses on social accommodation in the urban environment, where people's willingness to lend a helping hand to a needy fellow urbanite has become notoriously low. The study employs a paper-and-pencil measure of helping behavior, which permits recording people's responses to a range of different helping situations. Thus, it will be possible to systematically separate influences due to subjects' personal living experiences from those due to characteristics of the urban setting. We will see that the city's interpersonal coldness is not, as has often been assumed, a simple function of the urban dweller's insensitive nature. In fact, the reduced altruism of the city represents an active accommodation to urban reality based on a careful weighing of need, personal risk, and specific characteristics of the environment.

A DYNAMIC PICTURE OF SOCIAL ACCOMMODATION

Because the research studies in this section are highly diversified both environmentally and methodologically, it will again be useful to indicate some essential similarities in the process of social accommodation, which transcend each particular instance. Also, as social accommodation is a less dramatic process than environmental coping, this may aid the reader in noting the key characteristics of social accommodation to look for in reading this section. The underlying dynamic character of environmental coping is evidenced in two chief features: (1) the process is highly complex, and (2) the nature of the accommodation is quite unpredictable.

Complexity

One of the most compelling aspects of social accommodation is that, while the process appears at first to be quite simple, it characteristically evolves in a highly complex manner. This complexity may appear at the stage of weighing the antecedent conditions to accommodation. For example, the study of urban altruism reveals that the urbanite learns to weigh in a complex fashion both need and personal risk in determining the appropriateness of a helping response. Alternatively, complexity may be evident at the point of selecting the mode of the accommodating response, in that accommodation can evolve on a number of different levels or planes of social experience. In the psychiatric setting, for instance, accommodation occurs at both the quantitative and qualitative levels of social contact, while in the university counseling setting, accommodation is apparent on only the qualitative plane.

Unpredictability

The element of unpredictability in social accommodation is evidenced in its tendency to unfold in a subtle and rather surprising manner, at levels of social process where it is least anticipated. Social accommodation appears sometimes to evolve at less evident, more covert, underlying levels, while failing to develop at more evident and overt planes of social experience. For example, in the university counseling setting and to a lesser extent in the psychiatric environment, environmental users learn to maintain a moderately high level of overt interpersonal contact, while simultaneously and more subtly reducing dramatically the degree of intimacy in the exchange. The behavioral outcomes in each case represent carefully achieved, delicate balances between social response and environmental reality.

Unconscious

An additional characteristic of social accommodation, while less directly a dynamic element, must be noted as it is especially significant in terms of its broader social implications. Typically, the process occurs outside of human awareness. We will discover that environmental users themselves, even after demonstrating quite complex and subtle accommodations, are often totally unaware that the process has occurred. In effect, the human organism has become so adept at accommodating to environmental constraints that the complex social adjustments involved require neither explicit forethought nor conscious decision. Without even recognizing the response, environmental users reduce the intimacy, warmth, and depth of their interpersonal contacts to accommodate environmental demands. We will see that this lack of awareness of the accommodation process is especially evident in the psychiatric and university counseling settings. An important goal of this section is to make the reader more self-consciously aware of the process of social accommodation as it occurs in every-day life.

CHAPTER 5

Social Isolation and Seating Patterns in an Experimental Hospital Dayroom

The design of psychiatric hospitals has been subject to particular criticism for its failure to perform adequately as a social setting. A number of authors (Bailey, 1966; Griffin, Mauritzen, & Kasmar, 1969; Osmond, 1957) have underscored the need for environmental research to investigate psychiatric hospital settings in the light of psychological and social needs. Spivack (1967) has testified to the auditory and visual perceptual distortions caused by the elongated tunnels and corridors prevalent in many psychiatric facilities. Esser, Chamberlain, Chapple, and Kline (1965) have studied the relationship between territorial behavior on a psychiatric ward and position in a dominance hierarchy. Sivadon (1970) has reported favorable therapeutic results at the Marcel Rivière Institute in France where the architecture, size, and spatial relationship of buildings were designed to meet specific therapeutic objectives.

Although psychiatric patients spend considerable time in the ward dayroom, there is evidence to indicate that this setting tends to inhibit social interaction while coercing passive isolation (Hunter, Schooler, & Spohn, 1962; Ittelson, Proshansky, & Rivlin, 1970a; Sommer & Ross, 1958). Sommer and Ross (1958) have demonstrated a strong relationship between social behavior and seating patterns in the dayroom. In a Saskatchewan hospital, these investigators altered the dayroom seating arrangement from a sociofugal to a sociopetal pattern. Chairs that had previously been arranged shoulder-to-shoulder along the walls of the dayroom were moved closer together in small groups around tables. With the new furniture arrangement, social interaction among patients doubled in frequency.

AN INVESTIGATION IN AN EXPERIMENTAL DAYROOM

The purpose of the present study was to clarify further the effects of contrasting dayroom seating arrangements on the behavior of psychiatric patients. An *experimental* hospital dayroom was arranged to afford a setting where the effects of specific and controlled manipulations in seating could be observed on small groups of patients. Although a number of authors have criticized the physical environment of psychiatric hospitals as anti-therapeutic, there are few empirical data of sufficient rigor and specificity to permit hospital planners to make design decisions on the basis of scientific knowledge (Dyckman, 1966; Sanoff & Cohn, 1970).

Although the results in Sommer and Ross's study were attributed essentially to the change in seating patterns, a number of other simultaneous changes in the ward environment confound the clarity of this interpretation. For example, after seating patterns were changed to the more social arrangement, nurses "encouraged" the patients to sit at the tables and an occupational therapist began working on the ward. It seems probable that these two changes in the social setting of the ward may have induced some of the increased social participation among patients. Also, the tables on the ward were made more attractive by the introduction of flowers, vases, and more magazines during the second phase of the study. Again it appears possible that the change in the attractiveness of the ward may have contributed to the observed effects. Since seating patterns were changed in only one direction, i.e., no reversal procedure was employed, a "Hawthorne effect" was possible (cf. Higgs, 1970). In the present study such confounding factors were removed by manipulating seating patterns in a controlled experimental dayroom where hospital personnel did not participate in the setting and where furnishings and attractiveness of the room remained constant over experimental conditions. The possible confounding influence of a Hawthorne effect was avoided by assigning each experimental group to only one seating pattern.

In a hierarchical design (Myers, 1966), 120 subjects were randomly assigned to 20 six-member groups, and 5 groups were randomly assigned to each of four experimental conditions. The experimental conditions were as follows: *Sociofugal* — chairs were arranged shoulder-to-shoulder along the walls of the room; *Sociopetal* — chairs were arranged around two small tables in the

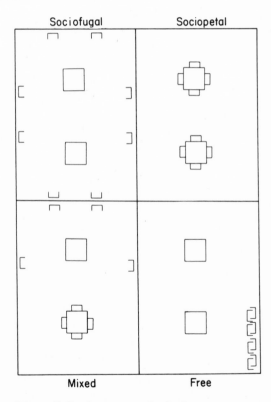

Figure 3. Seating patterns in the four treatments.

middle of the room; *Mixed* — chairs were arranged both along the walls and around a small table in the middle of the room; *Free* — patients were told to arrange the chairs themselves in any manner they wished. Figure 3 depicts visually the four experimental conditions.

Subjects were 120 hospitalized male psychiatric patients recruited from four unlocked wards at the Northampton Veterans Administration Hospital. Pilot observations had indicated that unsocial patients were not inclined to talk in any of the experimental settings. Therefore, patients for this study were selected by having the head nurse on each ward rank-order patients in terms of "how much time they spend talking with other patients on the ward." The list of patients on each ward was divided at the median, and subjects for the study were chosen by randomly selecting patients from the upper half of the distribution. This procedure necessarily limits inference from the present findings to the dayroom behavior of relatively social patients.

The experimental dayroom, which measured 9.15 m x 5.49 m, was furnished as follows: eight chairs, two tables (.91 m x .91 m), one circular stand in the center of the room, and eight standing ashtrays (one alongside each chair). Eight chairs were used to allow a relative degree of choice in chair selection. Chairs situated along the walls were 1.52 m apart side-by-side, 2.74 m apart corner-to-corner, and 3.66 m or 7.62 m apart face-to-face. Chairs situated at the tables were .91 m apart face-to-face and .76 m apart corner-to-corner. The following materials were placed on the stand: one pictorial magazine, one daily newspaper, two joke books, four decks of playing cards, one cribbage board, poker chips, checkers, one jigsaw puzzle, coffee, tea, donuts. A chair for an observer was located in an extended area of the room to the lower left and outside of the room area as depicted in Figure 3, 1.83 m from the nearest patient's chair. A heavy .91 m x 1.83 m table served both as a barrier between the observer and the patients and as a work space for the observer. A transistor radio on the observer's table played light music during the session.

To minimize interactions between types of hospital wards and the experimental settings, each experimental group was formed by taking three subjects from each of two different wards. Each group participated in one experimental condition for a 45-minute session. Systematic errors due to the time of day and time of month were avoided by matching conditions for time of day, and by running one group from each condition (in a random order) before repeating any condition. Chairs were arranged in their experimentally defined position before each session. Subjects entered the experimental settings as a group, and as soon as they entered the room, they were given the following instructions:

> We're interested in improving dayrooms for patients. We'd like patients to have a place where they can chat with one another, play some games, and generally do the things they'd like to do. We've set up this room especially for you to do those kinds of things. You're asked simply to remain in this room for one hour. While you're here you may have something to eat, chat with one another, play games, or do whatever else you'd like to do. The furniture has been specially arranged as it is. Please don't rearrange it. [Subjects in the Free condition were told they might put the furniture wherever they'd like in the room.] During the hour I'll be taking some notes, and I'd appreciate it if you wouldn't talk with me then. I won't be looking at particular people. I'm interested in how people in general would like to use a room like this. After the hour I'll be interested in your opinions about this room, and I'll be happy to answer any questions you have then. Some of you may not know one another. I'd like for each of you to give your first name and where you're from. [When patients finished introducing themselves] Fine, I'll let you know when the hour is up.

EXPERIMENTAL MEASURES

In a time-sampling procedure, each subject's behavior was recorded at 75-second intervals, moving from one subject to another in a predetermined rotating manner. This procedure resulted in 36 observations per subject. The behavior categories used in the study are defined in Table 6 and are based on the work of Harmatz, Mendelsohn, and Glassman (1970), Hunter et al., (1962), and Ittelson, Rivlin, and Proshansky (1970). Each subject was given a score in each category consisting of the total number of scores marked for the subject under that category during the

Table 6. Definition of Behavior Categories

Social
  Nonaggressive
    Verbal
      Conversation — verbal interaction between patients that was not a request
      or a response to a request concerning an object in the room.
      Games — comments between patients that were part of an ongoing game.
      Other — comments between patients that were requests or responses to
      requests concerning objects in the room, e.g., food or cigarettes.
    Nonverbal
      Games — playing, waiting turn, or setting up a social game.
      Other — exchanging of objects between patients, e.g., food or cigarettes.
  Aggressive
    Verbal — verbal threats or verbal abuse between patients.
    Nonverbal — physical assault or threatening gestures between patients
    (facial gestures were not scored).
Nonsocial
  Active — isolated game playing, eating, drinking, preparing food, reading or
  writing.
  Passive — sleeping or null behavior (null behavior was broadly defined to
  include walking, jiggling keys, lighting or smoking one's own cigarette, tying a
  shoe).
  Bizarre — talking to self, self-inflicted, deliberate injury, clearly unusual
  mannerisms or gestures.

---

session. Statistical analyses of behavior categories were of the
following two types: Planned comparisons (Hays, 1963) were used
to test the experimental hypotheses, and the analysis of variance
was used for post hoc analyses. The estimated variance for both the
t and F tests was the variability between groups within treatment
levels (Myers, 1966).

Two additional measures were collected after the behavioral
observations were completed. First, subjects were asked to
complete a semantic differential concerned with their perception of
the experimental settings. The following concepts were included
on the semantic differential scale: this room, the dayroom on my
ward, the other patients in this room, the other patients on my
ward, the observer in this room. The following scales were used:

three evaluative scales (clean–dirty, good–bad, fair–unfair), three potency scales (active–passive, hot–cold, fast–slow), and two novelty scales (new–old, unusual–usual). The standard instructions of Osgood, Suci, and Tannenbaum (1957) were used.

Second, the following unobtrusive measures (Webb, Campbell, Schwartz, & Sechrest, 1966) were taken: (1) Cigarette butts left in the room were counted; (2) the quantity of coffee consumed was measured; (3) the length of time patients remained in the experimental setting after the session had ended was recorded.

The reliability of the behavioral rating procedure was determined by having two independent observers simultaneously rate groups of subjects. Three separate reliability sessions were conducted, one before experimental data were collected, and two during the course of the study. A reliability score was calculated by dividing the number of times both observers agreed in each instance a behavior was rated by the total number of ratings. The reliability score in each of these sessions was 97%.

Table 7. **Mean Group Behavioral Scores**

	Experimental conditions			
Behavior categories[a]	Sociopetal	Mixed	Sociofugal	Free
Conversation[b]	61.8	40.8	32.0	16.8
Verbal games	14.6	9.6	.6	5.0
Other verbal	1.2	.4	.6	.4
Total verbal[c]	77.6	50.8	33.2	22.2
Nonverbal games	32.2	30.6	4.2	18.0
Other nonverbal	.6	.8	.6	0.0
Total nonverbal	32.8	31.4	4.8	18.0
Total social[c]	110.4	82.2	38.0	40.2
Nonsocial active	47.2	55.8	53.2	55.4
Nonsocial passive	77.8	87.6	123.2	120.6

[a] The categories of Aggressive and Bizarre behavior in which no behavior occurred are not shown.

[b] Significant at .05 level.
[c] Significant at .025 level.

DIMINISHED SOCIAL INTERACTION

Table 7 shows the mean number of behaviors per group recorded under each behavior category for the four experimental conditions.

Hypothesized Effects

It had been predicted that the Sociofugal setting would show less social interaction than would either the Sociopetal or the Mixed setting. The difference of 72.4 between the Sociofugal and Sociopetal settings was statistically significant at the .01 level with a one-tailed test (t = 2.60, df = 16), while the difference of 44.2 between the Sociofugal and Mixed settings was significant at the .025 level with a one-tailed test (t = 2.34, df = 16).* It had also been predicted that the Sociofugal setting would demonstrate less nonsocial activity than would either the Sociopetal or the Mixed setting. The very slight differences between settings in nonsocial activity were not statistically significant, and thus this prediction was not supported.

Free Setting

A surprising finding was that the Free setting showed markedly less social interaction than the Sociopetal and Mixed settings, and only slightly more social behavior than the Sociofugal setting. Although no strong predictions had been advanced concerning this setting, a general expectation had been that allowing patients to arrange their own seating would facilitate social interaction. The Free setting did not differ from the other settings in nonsocial

---

*The experimental data in six behavior categories exhibited significant heterogeneity of variance over conditions by Hartley's test, with the relationship between the means and the standard deviations of the treatments approximately proportional. For purposes of statistical analysis the data in all behavior categories were transformed by the logarithmic transformation $Y' = \log (Y + 1)$. The heterogeneity of variance was markedly decreased by the transformation, with only nonverbal behavior continuing to demonstrate significant heterogeneity of variance after transformation. The reported means are untransformed.

activity. Interestingly, 17 patients in the Free setting placed their chairs at the tables, in contrast to 12 patients who situated their chairs along the walls. In the Mixed setting, which permitted a relative degree of choice between sociopetal and sociofugal seating, 19 patients chose to sit at the table while 11 patients sat along the wall. Let us turn now to a closer analysis of social behavior over the four settings.

LOSS OF SELF-DIRECTION

The low level of social participation in the Free setting may in part have been due to the difficulties in social relationships that brought patients to the hospital, but was probably also a function of past training in the hospital environment itself. Sommer and Ross (1958) have labeled as "institutional sanctity" the feeling of both staff and patients in a hospital setting that the usual arrangement of furniture is necessarily good and unalterable. But in fact institutional sanctity goes far beyond the rigidity of furniture arrangements and pervades the character of the entire institution (cf. Goffman, 1961). Psychiatric patients have been consistently trained to be "outer-directed," while training for self-directed social encounter and environmental management — imperative adaptive skills outside of total institutions — has been greatly neglected. Environmental designers might play an important role in training psychiatric patients for self-direction by creating hospital environments that allow for graded experiences in environmental management (cf. Cumming & Cumming, 1962).

The finding that dayroom seating arrangements exert significant influence over patients' social behavior is most important in the light of the tendency of many professional mental health workers and of the public to attribute the psychiatric patient's behavior entirely to psychodynamic factors within himself. The most common response of ward nurses in this hospital on being told of this study was that chair arrangements would not affect patients' social functioning. "The patients may sit at the tables," one nurse responded confidently, "but they won't talk to one another." Sommer and Ross indicated a similar pessimism in hospital staff in the Saskatchewan hospital. Because of the tendency to underestimate the impact of furniture arrangements on behavior, when dayroom seating arrangements are thought about at all, it is with everyday staff needs rather than long-range therapeutic goals in mind. Typically, chairs are arranged in straight rows along the walls because this arrangement facilitates nurses surveying the ward and janitors sweeping the floor.

FURTHER SOCIAL IMPACTS

Verbal Interaction

The overall differences between settings in verbal interaction were statistically significant at the .025 level ($F = 4.31$, $df = 3/16$). The Sheffé multiple comparison procedure (Sheffé, 1959) was used to examine which treatments differed significantly from one another. This procedure indicated that the mean verbal interaction for the Sociopetal and Mixed conditions was significantly greater than the mean verbal interaction for the Sociofugal and Free conditions ($F = 3.56$, $df = 3/16$, $p < .025$).* Conversation accounted for 83% of the total verbal behavior in the experiment, compared to 16% for verbal games and only 1% for other verbal behavior. There was significantly more conversation over the total experiment than all other types of verbal behavior combined ($F = 20.85$, $df = 1/16$, $p < .001$).

Conversation

The treatment effect for conversation was statistically significant at the .05 level ($F = 3.40$, $df = 3/16$). The Sheffé multiple

*The Sheffé procedure also showed more verbal behavior in the Sociopetal setting than in the Free setting ($F = 2.84$, $df = 3/16$, $p < .10$), more verbal behavior in the Sociofugal setting than the mean of the Sociopetal and Mixed settings ($F = 2.78$, $df = 3/16$, $p < .10$), and more such behavior in the Sociopetal setting than the mean of the Sociofugal and Free settings ($F = 3.15$, $df = 3/16$, $p < .05$).

comparison procedure showed that mean conversation for the Sociopetal and Mixed conditions was significantly greater than mean conversation for the Sociofugal and Free conditions (F = 3.09, df = 3 / 16, p < .10). (Sheffé recommends an α level of .10 in using his multiple-comparison procedure.)

MORE SUBTLE EFFECTS

We have been concerned so far with a quantitative analysis of conversation over environmental settings, but there are also important qualitative differences between the types of conversation that developed in the Sociopetal and the Sociofugal settings. The following descriptive analysis is based on anecdotal comments recorded on the score sheets by the observer.

The sociopetal conversation was typified by an evenness of pace or flow, whether it involved two or more than two persons. It tended to continue unless an individual deliberately cut himself off from the conversation by leaving the group, lifting a newspaper in front of himself, or looking sharply to one side. This conversation, particularly when it involved more than two persons, was characterized by a great deal of energy or involvement, and was often marked by a high level of psychological closeness, trust, and intimacy. Typical topics of conversation included home visits, personal problems, service experiences, and finances. The sociopetal conversation was in many ways characterized by a quality of rapport that would have delighted any group leader. For example, in one sociopetal session, one patient talked about schizophrenia and another responded "I feel the same way, friend." In another sociopetal group, a patient talked about his adolescent son who had died recently, as another patient commented seriously, "That's sad."

The sociofugal conversation, in contrast, was marked by an unevenness of pace, proceeding in a sporadic manner. It was inclined to break off if the participants did not deliberately maintain it by sitting noticeably forward, resting on an elbow when conversing to one side, and maintaining constant eye contact. Typically, this conversation lacked the spontaneity and involvement of the sociopetal conversation. Topics of discussion in this conversation were rarely personal or intimate and typically involved food, baseball, dayroom activities, and past acquaintances in the hospital. The sociofugal conversation resembled the banter of casual acquaintances conversing simply to pass the time in a public setting.

UNOBTRUSIVE MEASURES

The scores for the Sociopetal and Mixed settings were greater than those for the Sociofugal and Free settings on all of the unobtrusive measures. These differences were statistically significant by the Mann-Whitney U Test on the Cigarette measure ($U = 1.5$, $n_1 = 7$, $n_2 = 8$, $p < .001$) and on the Coffee measure ($U = 8.5$, $n_1 = 7$, $n_2 = 8$, $p < .02$). It may be that cigarette and coffee consumption increased as a function of the greater social participation in the Sociopetal and Mixed settings. Raush, Dittman, and Taylor (1959) found that hospital settings in which food was present were characterized by greater interpersonal comfort and more positive social participation than were settings where there was no food. An alternative interpretation is that the greater consumption of coffee and cigarettes indicated a higher level of tension in the Sociopetal and Mixed settings. However, the tendency for patients to remain behind in these settings longer than in the others, and patients' generally favorable comments about these settings tend not to support the latter view.

LACK OF AWARENESS

The semantic differential failed to discriminate between experimental treatments on any of the concepts used in this study. There were also no significant differences between concepts when subjects were pooled over treatments. The lack of differences between conditions on the semantic differential was surprising in light of the marked behavioral differences between settings. Proshansky, Ittleson, and Rivlin (1970b) note that people are generally unaware of how their environment impinges on their lives, and it appears that patients in this study were not cognizant of the dramatic control the experimental settings exerted over their behavior.

SOME DESIGN IMPLICATIONS

How might the findings of this study be translated into practical and useful terms for the hospital designer interested in dayroom furniture arrangement? The most general implication is that the choice of seating patterns will affect the amount and the quality of social intercourse in the dayroom. A greater amount of conversation and psychologically closer and more intimate conversation will occur in sociopetal arrangements than in sociofugal ones. Also, multiperson conversations are more likely to develop in sociopetal settings. Allowing patients to arrange their own dayroom furniture appears to be unprofitable without prior training in self-directed environmental management. The change of hospital dayrooms from sociofugal patterns to sociopetal ones is practical and inexpensive, and the effects can be readily evaluated. Past tendencies to ignore the behavioral impact of physical settings and to perceive hospital environments as unalterable should not be allowed to present an insurmountable obstacle to productive and therapeutic environmental change.

Some qualifications to the present findings should also be noted. Sociopetal seating patterns cannot be expected to *create* social behavior among individuals who are not socially inclined. Pilot observations of unsocial patients in the Mixed arrangement indicated that social participation did not occur whether patients sat at the table or not. Sociopetal spaces do, however, play an important role in facilitating social interaction among socially inclined individuals. Sociofugal spaces, on the other hand, drastically inhibit social exchange, even between individuals who are socially inclined. Also future research dealing with dayroom seating patterns is needed to examine the effects of seating over a longer period of time with larger groups of patients. One might ask, for example, whether differences between contrasting settings will increase or diminish over extended periods of time, or if there is an optimal population density in dayrooms.

SUMMARY

The most important finding of this study was that seating patterns exerted a powerful control over the amount of social interaction among patients in a dayroom setting. The Sociofugal setting, as was predicted, demonstrated significantly less social interaction than did either the Sociopetal or the Mixed setting. It appears that social interaction will occur in settings where *some* seating is arranged in a sociopetal manner, while a setting that is totally sociofugal will dramatically suppress social participation. These findings in a controlled setting lend strong support to the position (Hall, 1969; Osmond, 1957, 1966; Sommer, 1967, 1969) that sociopetal spaces facilitate social interaction, while sociofugal spaces inhibit such interaction. The present results also support the findings of Sommer and Ross (1958) in an actual hospital dayroom. An unexpected finding was the very low level of social interaction in the Free setting. Of particular interest in terms of the process of social accommodation was that seating patterns affected not only the overall level of social contact but also the more subtle quality of social participation. The character of social interaction in the Sociofugal setting was less spontaneous, less intimate, and less warm than was socializing in the Sociopetal arrangement.

REFERENCES

Bailey, R. Needed: Optimum social design criteria. *The Modern Hospital*, 1966, *106*, 101–103.

Barker, R. G. Explorations in ecological psychology. *American Psychologist*, 1965, *20*, 1–15.

Cumming, J., & Cumming, E. *Ego and milieu*. New York: Atherton Press, 1962.

Dyckman, J. W. Environment and behavior: Introduction. *The American Behavioral Scientist*, 1966, *10*, 1-2.

Esser, A. H., Chamberlain, A. S., Chapple, E. D., & Kline, N. S. Territoriality of patients on a research ward. In J. Wortis (Ed.), *Recent Advances in Biological Psychiatry*, 1965, *7*, 35-44.

Field, H. H. *The environmental design implications of a changing health care system*. Paper presented at Environment and Cognition Conference, City University of New York, Graduate Center, June 1971.

Goffman, E. *Asylums: Essays on the social situation of mental patients and other inmates*. Garden City, New York: Anchor, 1961.

Griffin, W. V., Mauritzen, J. H., & Kasmar, J. V. The psychological aspects of the architectural environment: A review. *American Journal of Psychiatry*, 1969, *125*, 93-98.

Hall, E. T. *The hidden dimension*. New York: Doubleday, 1969.

Harmatz, M., Mendelsohn, R., & Glassman, M. *Naturalistic observation of hospitalized schizophrenic patients*. Unpublished manuscript, University of Massachusetts, 1970.

Hays, W. L. *Statistics for pyschologists*. New York: Holt, Rinehart & Winston, 1963.

Higgs, W. Reaction of schizophrenics to gross environmental change. *Journal of Abnormal Psychology*, 1970, *76*, 421-422.

Hunter, M., Schooler, C., & Spohn, H. E. The measurement of characteristic patterns of ward behavior in chronic schizophrenics. *Journal of Consulting Psychology*, 1962, *26*, 69-73.

Ittelson, W. H., Proshansky, H. M., & Rivlin, L. G. Bedroom size and social interaction of the psychiatric ward. *Environment and Behavior*, 1970, *2*, 255-270. (a)

Ittelson, W. H., Proshansky, H. M., & Rivlin, L. G. The environmental psychology of the psychiatric ward. In H. M. Proshansky, W. H. Ittelson, & L. G. Rivlin, (Eds.), *Environmental psychology: Man and his physical setting*. New York: Holt, Rinehart & Winston, 1970. (b)

Ittelson, W. H., Rivlin, L. G., & Proshansky, H. M. The use of behavioral maps in environmental psychology. In H. M. Proshansky, W. H. Ittelson, & L. G. Rivlin, (Eds.), *Environmental psychology: Man and his physical setting*. New York: Holt, Rinehart & Winston, 1970.

Izumi, K. Psychosocial phenomena and building design. *Building Research*, 1965, *2*, 9-11.

Lindheim, R. Factors which determine hospital design. *American Journal of Public Health*, 1966, *56*, 1668-1675.

Myers, J. L. *Fundamentals of experimental design*. Boston: Allyn and Bacon, 1966.

Osgood, C. E., Suci, G. J., & Tannenbaum, P. H. *The measurement of meaning*. Urbana: University of Illinois Press, 1957.

Osmond, H. Function as the basis of psychiatric ward design. *Mental Hospitals*, 1957, *8*, 23-30.

Proshansky, H. M., Ittelson, W. H., & Rivlin, L. G. Introduction. In H. M. Proshansky, W. H. Ittelson, & L. G. Rivlin (Eds.), *Environmental psychology: Man and his physical setting.* New York: Holt, Rinehart & Winston, 1970. (a)

Proshansky, H. M., Ittelson, W. H., & Rivlin, L. G. The influence of the physical environment on behavior: Some basic assumptions. In H. M. Proshansky, W. H. Ittelson, & L. G. Rivlin (Eds.), *Environmental psychology: Man and his physical setting.* New York: Holt, Rhinehart & Winston, 1970. (b)

Raush, H. L., Dittmann, A. T., & Taylor, T. J. Person, setting, and change in social interaction. *Human Relations,* 1959, *12,* 361–377.

Sanoff, H., & Cohn, S. Preface. In H. Sanoff, & S. Cohn, (Eds.), *Proceedings of the first annual environmental design research association conference.* Raleigh: North Carolina State University, 1970.

Scheffé, H. *The analysis of variance.* New York: Wiley, 1959.

Sivadon, P. Space as experienced: Therapeutic implications. In H. M. Proshansky, W. H. Ittelson, & L. G. Rivlin, (Eds.), *Environmental psychology: Man and his physical setting.* New York: Holt, Rinehart & Winston, 1970.

Sommer, R. Small group ecology. *Psychological Bulletin,* 1967, *67,* 145–152.

Sommer, R. *Personal space: The behavioral basis of design.* Englewood Cliffs, New Jersey: Prentice-Hall, 1969.

Sommer, R. & Ross, H. Social interaction on a geriatrics ward. *International Journal of Social Psychiatry,* 1958, *4,* 128–133.

Spivack, M. Sensory distortions in tunnels and corridors. *Hospital and Community Psychiatry,* 1967, January, 24–30.

Watson, D. Modeling the activity system. In H. Sanoff, & S. Cohn (Eds.), *Proceedings of the first annual environmental design research association conference.* Raleigh: North Carolina State University, 1970.

Webb, E. J., Campbell, D. T., Schwartz, R. D., & Sechrest, L. *Unobtrusive measures: Nonreactive research in the social sciences.* Chicago: Rand McNally, 1966.

Wohlwill, J. The emerging discipline of environmental psychology. *American Psychologist,* 1970, April, 303–312.

CHAPTER 6

Invasion of Privacy and Self-Disclosure in a Counseling Setting*

The cumulative influences of crowded settings, frenetically paced social life, and increasingly popular open-space design have made a sense of personal privacy progressively more difficult to achieve in contemporary society. A vital research question for the environmental psychologist concerns the extent to which social accommodation may be a psychological correlate of this reduced sense of privacy. An opportunity to investigate this issue in a particular setting emerged when we were approached by a counseling agency where, due to the constraints of restricted space, counselors were forced to operate in shared space in contrast to a private counseling room. Two questions were posed by the agency: (1) Would reduced privacy in the counseling setting adversely affect client self-disclosure? (2) If so, might an inexpensive environmental solution, such as the placement of a desk or book-case as a partial obstacle, increase self-disclosure?

WHAT WE KNOW ABOUT SELF-DISCLOSURE

Jourard (1964) has defined self-disclosure as the communication of any information about one's self that one person chooses to share

*The research discussed in this chapter was conducted in collaboration with Karl A. Slaikeu.

with another person. Over the last decade, self-disclosure as both
an interpersonal behavior and a personality construct has been
studied extensively as it operates in interpersonal relationships,
psychotherapy, and the laboratory (Cozby, 1973; Jourard, 1964,
1971). In a recent review of self-disclosure research, Cozby (1973)
has proposed that investigation include other factors that may
restrict self-disclosure, such as the need for privacy. An important
related question concerns the effect of invasion of privacy on self-
disclosure. There has been no previous research, however, dealing
with the relationship between self-disclosure and degree of privacy,
though earlier work in a number of related areas is of relevance.

While there has been no previous research dealing with the
relationship between self-disclosure and invasion of privacy, an
assumption of a potential negative relationship is compelling.
Westin (1967) in describing a number of features of privacy has
described *intimacy* as the situation where an individual acts as a
part of a small social unit that claims group seclusion in order to
achieve relaxed and frank interpersonal relationships within the
group. The level of self-disclosure by an interviewee toward an
interviewer of recognized position and status should be severely
restricted when the intimacy of the interview situation is invaded
by a third party whose presence is not legitimized.

A small body of work has accumulated which demonstrates
that self-disclosure is under situational control. Self-disclosure in a
social dyad has been demonstrated to be increased under conditions
of isolation (Altman & Haythorne, 1965), and to be positively
related to the degree of compatibility between members of the dyad
(Taylor, Altman, & Sorrentino, 1969). Additional research has
investigated reciprocity in self-disclosure between members of an
interacting dyad (Chittick & Himelstein, 1967; Erlich & Graven,
1971) and level of self-disclosure in small group settings as a
function of group atmosphere and cohesiveness (Johnson &
Ridener, 1974). McCall (1970) has postulated an increasing
gradation of self-disclosure in relation to the rooms of the home,
moving from the kitchen through the living room, to the bedroom.

Some social psychological research has examined the effects of
invasion of privacy on factors other than self-disclosure. Research

in libraries and cafeterias (Felipe & Sommer, 1966; Sommer, 1969) has indicated that invasion of personal space is experienced as aversive and typically results in flight from the situation. However, this research has been restricted to one individual invading the personal space of another individual and has not studied the effects of invasion either on a social dyad or on interpersonal verbal behavior. Some research evidence suggests that the negative effects of invasion of privacy may be decreased through the use of partitions. Baum, Reiss, and O'Hara (1974) have noted that partitions can increase psychological comfort in spaces otherwise overloaded. Holahan and Saegert (1973) found that partitions installed in previously multibed hospital dormitories resulted in a more personalized use of the space by patients. More generally, Desor (1972) has suggested a social norm connoting that an invader on the opposite side of any physical feature that implied segregation can be effectively ignored or psychologically filtered out.

A LABORATORY ANALOGUE

The design of the present study involved a laboratory analogue simulating the real life situation where an invasion of privacy by a third party occurs in a counseling interview. A laboratory analogue was chosen in order to achieve a higher level of experimental control than would be possible in a real life setting. This allowed for a controlled invasion of privacy, controlled manipulation of an environmental feature (a spatial divider), and a standardized interview procedure. In addition, in accord with Cozby's (1973) recommendations of the use of behavioral measures of self-disclosure, the design facilitated the collection of a behavioral measure of self-disclosure by tape-recording the interview.

The type of spatial divider investigated was three feet in height in order to simulate a perceptual boundary around the interacting dyad without actually blocking visual access. This type of divider was selected over other design alternatives for a number of reasons. At a practical level, since only limited remodeling funds were available to the counseling agency, a demonstration that a partial screen could achieve increased privacy would be especially useful. The dividers were similar to the solid base section of the type of partition often used in office settings. At a more general level, architectural consultants we contacted were especially interested in investigating the application of such a partial screen as a means of increasing a sense of personal privacy through simulating the perception of a personal space boundary.

The experimental situation involved an interviewer interviewing a naive subject concerning a number of personal issues that called for a moderate to high degree of self-disclosure. All interviewers were blind to the experimental hypotheses. A total of four interviewers, balanced over experimental conditions, was used to restrict effects due to type of interviewer. The design included the three following experimental conditions: Private — the interviewer and subject were alone in the interview setting. Invasion — a third party (an experimental confederate) invaded the dyadic interview by entering the room and remaining through-out the interview. Spatial Divider — a third party again invaded the interview; however, three-foot-high spatial dividers were placed around both the interviewing dyad and the intruder to enhance the perception of privacy. To avoid systematic effects due to sex, two male and two female interviewers and invaders were used, who were balanced over experimental conditions. Two types of experimental measures were collected: (1) behavioral — the inter-view was tape-recorded and later coded using three operational measures of self-disclosure; and (2) self-report — subjects com-pleted a postsession questionnaire evaluating the experimental situation.

Subjects in the study were 74 volunteers from the Introductory Psychology course at the University of Texas. Twenty-two subjects were males and 52 subjects were females. The majority of sub-jects were university freshmen, with the remainder typically sophomores. Subjects were randomly assigned to experimental conditions, with 25 subjects in the Private and Spatial Divider conditions and 24 subjects in the Invasion condition.

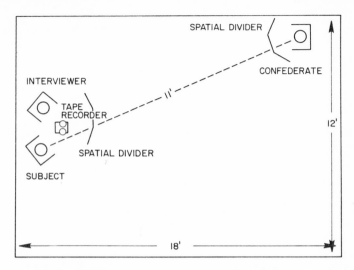

Figure 4. Experimental setting in Spatial Divider condition.

All experimental conditions were conducted in the same room, which was painted a soft blue and was attractively decorated, with books, nicknacks, and pictures on the walls. All furnishings, with the exception of the spatial dividers, remained constant in both type and location over the three experimental conditions. The only difference in the room in physical design over the experimental conditions was that the spatial dividers were present in the Spatial Divider condition and absent in both the Private and Invasion conditions. Figure 4 depicts the experimental setting in the Spatial Divider condition.

INTERVIEWING STUDENTS

Interview and Postsession Tests

The interview procedure and postsession testing were conducted in exactly the same manner over all experimental conditions. After seating the subject, the interviewer stated:

> We're developing a number of different interview scales. I'm going to
> ask you a range of questions and I'd like you to answer as openly and
> honestly as possible. The tape recorder is simply for us to compare
> different scales later on. All of your comments are con-
> fidential — your name will not be on the tape. Also, you don't have to
> answer any questions you'd rather not, OK?

Next the interviewer turned on the tape recorder and initiated the
interview. In the interview, the interviewer asked subjects to
respond to 14 questions ranging from low to high intimacy. Four of
these questions were selected on an *a priori* basis for self-disclosure
coding, with two questions of moderate intimacy value and two
questions of high intimacy value. The moderate intimacy value
questions were: (1) "What problems did you face in adjusting to
living away from home?" (2) "What problems did you have in first
meeting new guys (girls) at Texas?" The high intimacy value
questions were: (1) "What personal characteristics do you have
that you feel anxious about in social situations?" (2) "Do you ever
worry about how attractive you are to the opposite sex? In what
way?" During the interview, the interviewer made minimal
prompts, which included: "Hmm, okay, I see, yes." After
completing the interview, the interviewer turned off the tape
recorder and stated:

> I have a short survey for you to fill out. It is anonymous, so don't put
> your name on it. When you are finished, seal it in this envelope and
> deposit it in the box outside the door.

The interviewer then handed the subject the postsession tests and
left the room while the subject completed the forms. When the
subject had finished the postsession material, the subject was
debriefed and dismissed.

Confederate

When the experimental confederate was present (i.e., in the
Invasion and Spatial Divider conditions), the following additional
procedure was followed. The confederate arrived at the testing
room at the same time as the subject, posing as a subject for the

experiment. After first greeting the subject, the interviewer turned to the confederate and asked: "Are you here for experiment number 83?" After the confederate answered affirmatively, the interviewer stated: "Okay, here's what I'll do. [To the subject] I'll interview you first, and while you're waiting, [to the confederate] I have a survey for you to fill out." The interviewer then seated the subject in the dyadic seating arrangement and, handing the confederate a form, asked him to be seated in the chair across the room. While the subject was being interviewed, the confederate worked quietly on the test materials, spending about 50% of the time writing and 50% of the time looking toward the subject.

MEASURING SELF-DISCLOSURE

Three independent measures of self-disclosure were used. Two judges were used, a male and a female undergraduate, who were blind to both the purpose of the study and the experimental condition in which each tape was recorded. The judges were trained in the scoring procedure during five hours of practice sessions using tapes from a pilot study, and interrater reliability averaged 90% across the three measures.

1. *Total Response Time.* The number of seconds that elapsed from the time the interviewer finished asking the questions to when the interviewer began the next question (i.e., the amount of time the subject took in responding) was recorded for each of the four questions. A total response time score for each subject was calculated by adding the number of seconds for the four responses.

2. *Haymes Score.* Responses were coded using Haymes's techniques for measuring self-disclosure from taped interviews (cf. Jourard, 1971, pp. 216–218). The Haymes technique measures expressions of emotion, need, fantasies, and self-awareness, giving higher scores to expressions when they are in the first person (score equals 2) than when they are in third person (score equals 1) or third person reflexive (score equals 0). Scores for the four items were added to yield a total Haymes score for each subject.

3. *Weighted Score for Subjects of Clauses and Sentences.* A

limitation of the Haymes scoring system is that it scores only emotionally laden material. A third measure was developed to reflect subject's speech style, i.e., statements about one's self versus statements about "people in general," across the entire response. For each of the four responses, the number of first person and third person utterances was counted. (Second person utterances were so infrequent as not to warrant counting.) First person utterances were given a weight of 2 and third person utterances a weight of 1. Scores for each item were added yielding a total weighted score for each subject.

Each subject completed a postsession questionnaire concerned with the subject's attitudes toward the experimental room and toward the interviewer. The questionnaire consisted of eight items, which were composed of polar opposite adjectives rated along a 7-point scale. The items were grouped into two subscales: (1) a *Privacy* scale measured the subject's perception of the degree of privacy in the experimental room, and (2) an *Affect* scale measured the subject's perception of positive affect on the part of the interviewer. The Privacy scale was composed of three items: private–nonprivate, comfortable–uncomfortable, personal–impersonal. The Affect scale was composed of five items: involved–uninvolved, tight–relaxed, warm–cold, unempathic–empathic, likable–unlikable.

SOCIAL ACCOMMODATION: A REDUCTION OF SELF-DISCLOSURE

Table 8 summarizes the three behavioral measures of self-disclosure for the three experimental conditions, including mean scores in each condition and results of the one-way analyses of variance. The overall differences between experimental conditions were statistically significant on the Haymes ($p < .03$) and Weighted Score ($p < .04$) measures. Self-disclosure was higher in the Private condition than in either the Invasion or Spatial Divider conditions on all three measures. Surprisingly, self-disclosure in the Invasion condition was slightly greater than in the Spatial Divider condition.

Table 8. Behavioral Measures of Self-Disclosure in the Three Experimental Conditions

| | Experimental condition | | | | | | ANOVA | | |
| | Private | | Invasion | | Spatial divider | | | | |
Variable	X̄	SD	X̄	SD	X̄	SD	F	df[a]	p
Total response time	83.91	55.30	68.63	55.76	58.86	22.25	1.56	2/59	.22
Haymes score	3.27	2.07	1.84	1.83	1.90	1.97	3.58	2/59	.03
Weighted score	20.00	16.09	13.36	12.88	10.05	7.74	3.39	2/59	.04

[a]Twelve tapes ranging across all conditions could not be coded due to recording difficulties.

The Scheffé (1959) multiple-comparison procedure was used to test the significance of differences between the experimental conditions, and revealed that the significant difference was between the Private and the other two conditions. On the Haymes measure there was significantly more self-disclosure in the Private condition than in the Invasion condition ($F = 5.92$, $df = 2/59$, $p < .10$), and in the Private condition than in the average of the Invasion and Spatial Divider conditions ($F = 7.69$, $df = 2/59$, $p < .05$). (Scheffé recommends an α level of .10 in using his multiple-comparison procedure.) For the Weighted Score measure, there was again significantly more self-disclosure in the Private condition than in the Spatial Divider condition ($F = 6.13$, $df = 2/59$, $p < .10$), and in the Private condition than in the average of the Spatial Divider and the Invasion conditions ($F = 5.99$, $df = 2/59$. $p < .10$).

A COMPLEX PICTURE OF ACCOMMODATION

What is especially compelling about these findings in terms of the process of social accommodation is their complexity and subtlety. In effect, while the total amount of time subjects talked in each setting did not differ significantly, the *content* of what they chose to talk about varied dramatically. In the private condition,

Table 9. Self-Report Measures for Subjects in the Three Experimental Conditions

	Experimental condition								
	Private		Invasion		Spatial divider		ANOVA		
Scale	$\bar{X}$	SD	$\bar{X}$	SD	$\bar{X}$	SD	F	df	p
Privacy	11.8	3.96	9.3	3.01	11.0	3.89	3.16	2/71	.05[a]
Affect	26.4	3.74	28.3	4.69	26.9	3.82	1.70	2/71	.18

[a]Statistically significant at .05 level.

respondents discussed their own personal experiences in an immediate and personally relevant way. In both situations where their privacy was invaded, in contrast, students reduced the degree of personal immediacy of their responses and talked instead about the experiences of third parties or people in general. Thus, while maintaining a generally cooperative and responsive demeanor toward the interviewer in all three circumstances, subjects simultaneously and quite subtly altered the nature of their interchange to accommodate the very real constraints of the environmental context within which they found themselves.

LACK OF AWARENESS

Data from subjects' postsession questionnaires indicated, again, the extent to which the process of social accommodation may occur outside of conscious awareness. For the Spatial Divider condition, an interesting discrepancy emerged between students' verbal reports and their actual environmental behavior. Table 9 summarizes the data from subjects' postsession questionnaires for the three experimental conditions, including mean scores in each condition and results of the one-way analyses of variance. Overall differences between experimental conditions on the Privacy scale were statistically significant at the .05 level. Subjects in the Private condition rated the room as most private, while those in the Invasion condition rated it as least private. Subjects in the Spatial Divider condition rated the room as only slightly less private than did those in the Private condition. The Scheffé multiple-comparison procedure was again used to test the significance of differences between the experimental conditions and indicated that the significant difference was between the Invasion and the other two conditions. The mean score in the Private condition was significantly more positive than the mean score in the Invasion condition ($F = 5.50, df = 2/71, p < .10$). Also, the mean score in the Invasion condition was significantly less positive than the average score in the Private condition and the Spatial Divider condition ($F = 5.14, df = 2/71, p < .10$). Thus, the questionnaire data revealed that, although the Spatial Divider condition was characterized by less self-disclosure behavior, subjects were not consciously aware of the reduced privacy in that setting.

WHY THE DIVIDERS FAILED

It is compelling to speculate why the spatial dividers in this study failed to increase, and, in fact, may actually have further decreased, self-disclosure. An immediate interpretation is that the size of the dividers was too small and did not afford an adequate buffer to screen out effectively the invader. Desor's (1972) contention that any physical feature that suggests segregation can effectively screen an invader may be too broad. Also, it is possible that the presence of the dividers may have further sensitized subjects to both the appropriateness of privacy in the situation and the fact that adequate privacy was not actually achieved. However, the fact that subjects did perceive the Spatial Divider condition as more private than the Invasion condition suggests that the full explanation may not reside in the nature of the spatial dividers themselves. Let us examine an interesting alternative explanation.

COPING AND ACCOMMODATION BY THE
INTERVIEWERS

An exciting alternative view of the present findings is that the spatial dividers were at least partially effective, but that the behavior of the interviewers themselves was affected by the dividers! In fact, two sources of data indicate that the interviewers engaged in aspects of both environmental coping and social accommodation during the experiment. First, subjects rated the interviewer's affect as more positive in the Invasion condition than in either of the other two conditions (Table 9). Apparently, challenged by the poor environmental circumstances of the Invasion condition, the interviewers coped by working harder to establish emotional rapport between themselves and the subjects. In addition, further examination of the tapes revealed that the number of prompts given by the interviewers was more than twice as high in both the Private and Invasion conditions as in the Spatial Divider condition. It seems that the interviewers may have, in effect, "fallen down on the job," pulling less hard for fuller responses, when they felt an environmental prop was available to facilitate interpersonal rapport.

This interpretation suggests what we might consider an environmentally stimulated "performance inversion." That is, under some circumstances people may work harder under less than ideal environmental conditions, while relaxing somewhat in less challenging situations. This view is congruent with a recent view of environment–behavior systems propounded by Altman and Taylor (1973). They have coined the term *social penetration* to convey the notion that interpersonal interaction involves simultaneously both verbal and nonverbal exchange, and *active use* of the *physical environment*. If we add a balance component to this model of the environment–behavior system, it is reasonable to speculate that as one feature of the system (e.g., physical environment) fosters a greater level of intimacy, a different feature (e.g., verbal behavior) is adapted downward in order to sustain an overall level of intimacy appropriate to the dyad. Moos (1975) has, in addition, proposed that individual potential may be maximally enhanced in environmental settings that are "optimally incongruent." That is, human growth may achieve its fullest expression under environmental conditions that are both challenging and obtainable. The notion of such a "performance inversion" presents an especially exciting realm of investigation for further research in environmental psychology.

SOME IMPLICATIONS FOR COUNSELING

What are the implications of this study for the counseling agency concerned about the facilitative effectiveness of its counselors under shared space conditions? First, the present results in an analogue situation demonstrate that an invasion of counseling privacy will impede facilitative effectiveness through lowering client self-disclosure. Of course, generalization of these findings to a real counseling setting, where the client is seeking help or where an invader may be sanctioned by the counselor, should be cautious. Second, the findings indicate that the strategic placement of partial barriers, such as desks or bookcases, will not *alone* enhance self-disclosure. Effective utilization of physical props will necessitate that attention be given to their influences on both clients and counselors. In practice, good environmental design solutions will need to proceed concomitantly with staff training on how to most effectively use new environmental features.

SUMMARY

The results of this study in an analogue situation demonstrate that reduced privacy decreased client self-disclosure in a counseling setting. The findings also indicate that a partial screen, as might be provided by a desk or a bookcase, while sufficient to affect the client's perception of privacy, will not positively increase the level of self-disclosure. Self-disclosure was, as expected, greater in private than in nonprivate conditions. However, surprisingly, self-disclosure was less in an invasion of privacy condition where spatial dividers were employed than in one in which dividers were not used. A subtle aspect of social accommodation involved the finding that, although counselees were quite verbal in the invasion of privacy situation, the personal "immediacy" of their conversation was considerably reduced relative to more private circumstances. Of particular interest was the discovery that the behavior of the interviewers themselves was altered by the experimental manipulations. It appeared that the interviewers worked harder under poor environmental conditions, while tending to "fall down on the job" under less challenging circumstances.

REFERENCES

Altman, I., & Haythorne, W. W. Interpersonal exchange in isolation. *Sociometry*, 1965, *32*, 411–426.

Altman, I., & Taylor, D. A. *Social penetration: The development of interpersonal relationships*. New York: Holt, Rinehart & Winston, 1973.

Baum, A., Reiss, M., & O'Hara, J. Architectural variants of reaction to spatial invasion. *Environment and Behavior*, 1974, *6*, 91–100.

Chittick, E. F., & Himelstein, P. The manipulation of self-disclosure. *Journal of Psychology*, 1967, *65*, 117–121.

Cozby, P. C. Self-disclosure: A literature review. *Psychological Bulletin*, 1973, *79*, 73–91.

Desor, J. A. Toward a psychological theory of crowding. *Journal of Personality and Social Psychology*, 1972, *21*, 79–83.

Erlich, H. J., & Graven, D. B. Reciprocal self-disclosure in a dyad. *Journal of Experimental Social Psychology*, 1971, *7*, 389–400.

Felipe, N. J., & Sommer, R. Invasions of personal space. *Social Problems*, 1966, *14*, 206–211.

Holahan, C. J., & Saegert, S. Behavioral and attitudinal effects of large-scale variation in the physical environment of psychiatric wards. *Journal of Abnormal Psychology*, 1973, *82*, 454–462.

Johnson, D. L., & Ridener, L. R. Self-disclosure, participation, and perceived cohesiveness in small group interaction. *Psychological Reports*, 1974, *35*, 361–362.

Jourard, S. M. *The transparent self*. Princeton, New Jersey: Van Nostrand, 1964.

Jourard, S. M. *Self-disclosure: An experimental analysis of the transparent self*. New York: Wiley, 1971.

McCall, G. J. (Ed.). *Social relationships*. Chicago, Illinois: Aldine, 1970.

Moos, R. H. *Evaluating and changing community settings*. Paper presented at annual meeting of the American Psychological Association, Chicago, 1975.

Scheffé, H. *The analysis of variance*. New York: Wiley, 1959.

Sommer, R. *Personal space: The behavior basis of design*. Englewood Cliffs, New Jersey: Prentice-Hall, 1969.

Taylor, D. A., Altman, I., & Sorrentino, R. Interpersonal exchange as a function of rewards and cost and situational factors: Expectancy confirmation-disconfirmation. *Journal of Experimental Social Psychology*, 1969, *5*, 324–339.

Westin, A. F. *Privacy and freedom*. New York: Atheneum, 1967.

CHAPTER 7

The Unresponsive Urbanite: Personal versus Situational Determinants

The urbanite, according to popular stereotype, is regarded as more socially aloof and less interpersonally responsive and helpful than the rural dweller. Widespread media reaction to the killing of Kitty Genovese within view of 38 passive residents in her New York City neighborhood encouraged an interest on the part of social psychologists in the phenomenon of the "unresponsive bystander" (cf. Latane & Darley, 1970). To date, however, social psychological knowledge in this area has been inconclusive and contradictory.

In general, earlier studies tended to support the popular view of the unresponsive urbanite (Clarke & Word, 1972; Merrens, 1973; Milgram, 1970; Morgan, 1973). Later research, however, has indicated no effect in altruism due to community size (Korte, 1975; Lesk & Zippel, 1975) or even that urban dwellers are more helpful than their rural counterparts (Schneider & Mockus, 1974; Weiner, 1976). Milgram (1970), in a widely quoted paper, proposed a conceptual framework for explaining the early findings reporting less helping in city than town. He contended that the urbanite, in adapting to stimulus overload caused by large numbers of people and high levels of heterogeneity and density, developed generalized social norms curtailing and minimizing both the breadth and intensity of social contacts. Thus, while research data in this area remain equivocal, the earlier and most widely disseminated findings have tended to support the stereotype that the city dweller is less altruistic than the rural resident.

Most importantly, independent of the direction of the effect, the general thrust of almost all of this previous work has been toward person-centered interpretations of urban–rural differences in altruism. In fact, however, no previous research has adequately addressed an essential underlying issue: to what extent are differences in helping behavior a function of *personal* differences in terms of urban–rural background, which are generalizable over settings, and to what extent are they a function of *situational* differences between urban and rural environments, which are stable across personal backgrounds. In field studies, conducted in contrasting urban and rural areas, personal and situational variables have been confounded since only urbanites have been studied in the city and only ruralites in the country. In laboratory studies, using a staged helping event, urban–rural differences in personal background have been legitimately examined at the expense of any information concerning situational effects that can be readily generalized to naturalistic settings. A growing body of literature, which has systematically investigated personal versus situational determinants of social behavior (Bem & Allen, 1974; Ekehammar, 1974; Endler & Hunt, 1968; Mischel, 1973; Price & Bouffard, 1974), has consistently found that both variables and especially their interactions are of importance. At a practical level, Caplan and Nelson (1973) have lamented the negative social consequences of psychologists' proclivity to ascribe exclusively person-centered causal attributions in analyzing social problems.

A SURVEY STUDY

The purpose of the present study was to systematically examine the relative importance of situational variables, personal variables, and their interactions as determinants of judged appropriateness of altruistic behavior along the urban–rural dimension. The measure of judged appropriateness of altruistic behavior was taken from Price and Bouffard (1974). This measure was selected because it had been developed specifically to examine personal versus situational effects on social behavior and because it was especially appropriate to investigating possible normative differences in altruistic responses between city and country as suggested by Milgram (1970). Personal variables investigated included size of the subject's home town and sex. Situational variables included the urban–rural dimension of the helping environment, and two characteristics of the helping request. The requests varied both the urgency of the request and the degree of personal risk involved in helping. The requests were selected to allow comparison with field observations of helping behavior in previous studies reported by Milgram (1970), which employed similar helping situations.

Subjects were 173 introductory psychology students who fulfilled a course requirement by their participation. The sample included 87 males and 86 females. Subjects were divided into three groups on the basis of the population size of their home town: *small* — less than 50,000 ($N = 47$); *medium* — 50,000 to 500,000 ($N = 57$); *large* — greater than 500,000 ($N = 69$).

HELPING SCALE

Subjects were administered a scale that measured their judgment of the appropriateness of helping responses across two contrasting helping environments and four different helping requests. Administration of the scale was in a group format, with approximately 60 subjects in each of three testing sessions, and the scale required approximately 30 minutes for completion. Instructions for the measure of judged appropriateness were as follows:

> From various sources in our everyday life we have all developed a subjective "impression" or "feeling" for the appropriateness of any given behavior in a particular situation. The judgments about appropriateness may not always be "rational" or "logical" but they are a very real part of all of us. In this experiment, we are interested in your judgment of the appropriateness of some particular behaviors in some particular situations. Your task in each case is simply to rate, on a scale from 0 to 9, the appropriateness of the particular behavior in the situation given. The rating scale is weighted as follows: 0 = The

behavior is extremely inappropriate in this situation. 9 = The
behavior is extremely appropriate in this situation. Altogether you
will be asked to rate four different behaviors across a number of
different situations. The behaviors will be presented one at a time,
and will be followed by a list of situations. After each situation, *mark
an "X"* at the place on the scale that best describes your judgment of
the appropriateness of the particular behavior in that particular
situation. You should view each situation separately, considering it
independently from the ratings you give to other situations.

Settings

The scale presented the subject with two contrasting environmental settings, comparing a typical large city with a typical small
midwestern town. They read as follows:

1. You are a resident of a large city, such as New York, Philadelphia,
   or Los Angeles.
2. You are a resident of a small town (less than one thousand
   residents) in the Midwest.

Requests

Four different helping requests were presented for each of the
environmental settings. The requests were chosen to vary the
dimensions of personal *risk* (a face-to-face vs. a telephone contact)
and *urgency* of the request (a disabled vehicle vs. looking for a
friend). They read as follows:

1. You are at home alone in the late afternoon, and a stranger, who is
   a male about 25 years old, knocks at your door. He tells you that his
   car has broken down nearby. He asks if you will allow him to come
   in to use your phone to call his garage. You are to rate how
   appropriate you feel it would be to allow him in to use your phone
   in each of the following situations.
2. You are at home alone in the late afternoon, and a stranger, who is
   a male about 25 years old, knocks at your door. He tells you that he
   has misplaced the address of a friend who lives nearby. He asks if
   you would allow him to come in to use your phone to call his friend.
   You are to rate how appropriate you feel it would be to allow him
   to use your phone in each of the following situations.
3. You are at home alone in the late afternoon, and receive a phone
   call from a stranger, who is a male about 25 years old. He tells you

he is calling from a parkway, and using his last dime, has reached
you accidentally through dialing a wrong number. He asks if you
will call his auto garage (he gives you the garage's number), and
tell them that his car has broken down, stranding him on the
parkway, and that he needs a repair truck. You are to rate how
appropriate you feel it would be to phone the garage and leave the
message in each of the following situations.

4. You are at home alone in the late afternoon, and receive a phone
call from a stranger, who is a male about 25 years old. He tells you
that he is calling from a parkway, and using his last dime, has
reached you accidentally through dialing a wrong number. He asks
if you will call his friend (he gives you the friend's number) to let
him know that he will be arriving about 30 minutes late. You are to
rate how appropriate you feel it would be to phone the friend and
leave the message in each of the following situations.

The settings and requests were presented in a randomized
order and were counterbalanced over each half of the sample.

Additional Measures

The scale also measured subjects' *fear* for personal safety in the city.
Measurement was again along a 9-point scale. This item read as
follows:

> For the following opinion about large cities indicate how
> characteristic or uncharacteristic of yourself you feel the opinion is.
> Large cities are unattractive places to live because of their high crime
> rate, constant fear concerning personal safety, and dangerous streets
> and neighborhoods.

Finally, to measure size of *home town*, subjects were asked to
indicate the name and population size of the city or town where
they resided for the longest period of time before coming to the
university. The reported population was verified in an atlas and
corrected where necessary.

URBAN-RURAL EFFECTS ON ALTRUISM

Data were analyzed in a 5-factor analysis of variance with judged
appropriateness of helping as the dependent variable. The

personal variables (home town and sex) were between-groups variables and the situational variables (urban–rural differences, urgency, and risk) were within-groups variables. (To simplify the analysis and to reduce the probability of type I errors, only main effects and two-way interactions were examined in the analysis of variance.)

Main Effects

All three situational variables yielded highly significant main effects at the .0001 level ($df = 1/67$). The F values for these main effects were: urban–rural difference, $F = 250.48$; urgency, $F = 31.17$; risk, $F = 359.00$. Mean judged appropriateness of altruistic responses in the "large city, such as New York, Philadelphia, or Los Angeles" was 4.37 compared to 6.46 in the small midwestern town. Subjects were more inclined to respond altruistically to the individual with the disabled vehicle ($\overline{X} = 5.72$) than the individual seeking a friend ($\overline{X} = 5.12$). Personal risk demonstrated a particularly strong effect, with the phone caller receiving a mean score of 7.15 and the person at the door only 3.68. For the personal variables, sex showed a significant main effect ($F = 15.95$, $df = 1/167$, $p < .0001$), with males ($\overline{X} = 5.90$) more altruistic than females ($\overline{X} = 4.93$). Home town background failed to yield a significant main effect, although, interestingly, subjects from large city backgrounds were the most altruistic group ($\overline{X}$ for large home town = 5.67, $\overline{X}$ for medium home town = 5.24, $\overline{X}$ for small home town = 5.34).

Interactions

Two interactions involving risk were significant, urban–rural difference × risk and sex × risk, at the .0001 level ($df = 1/167$). The F values for these interactions were: urban–rural difference × risk, $F = 57.31$; sex × risk, $F = 61.38$. Altruism was especially low in the large city environment under the high risk situation. While females were slightly more altruistic than males in the low risk situation, they were markedly less so under high risk. In addition, one interaction involving home town showed a statistical trend, ($F = 2.64$, $df = 2/167$, $p < .08$), home town ×urban–rural difference. The home town interaction was complex. While all three home town groups responded more altruistically in the Midwest than in the large city and subjects from large city backgrounds were most altruistic in both environments, the relative difference between the large city groups and the other two groups was greater in the large city than in the Midwest environment.

URBAN FEAR

A simple analysis of variance was run with home town as the independent variable and fear of the city as the dependent variable. A significant main effect was found for the fear measure ($F = 10.86$, $df = 2/170$, $p < .0001$). Small and medium town subjects demonstrated higher levels of fear of the city than large city subjects.

SOCIAL ACCOMMODATION IN THE CITY

These findings provide strong evidence in support of the popular stereotype that urban settings are characterized by less willingness to lend a helping hand than are rural environments. Across all sizes of home town background, subjects were dramatically less inclined to offer interpersonal assistance in the large city than in the small town setting. These results are, in addition, consistent with a number of previous studies (Clarke & Word, 1972; Merrens, 1973; Milgram, 1970; Morgan, 1973), which have demonstrated that altruistic behavior is lower in city than town. The present findings, however, also raise a number of important issues concerning the *character* of social accommodation in the city. In fact, they point unmistakably to the dynamic nature of accommodation in urban life, underscoring both the complexity and adaptive aspect of the accommodation process.

INTERACTIONAL COMPLEXITY

In the light of the present results, social accommodation in the city emerges as an especially complex process. This is particularly true for the personal variables, which proved less important as main effects than when viewed in interaction with situational variables. For example, while no main effect was found for size of home town background, home town interacted with the urban–rural setting dimension (statistical trend) in affecting altruism. In general, while all subjects responded less altruistically in city than town, those from large city backgrounds were relatively more altruistic in the city than were subjects from midsized and small home towns. In addition, degree of personal risk demonstrated important inter-actions with both the urban–rural dimension and sex in influencing altruism. The urban–rural effect was markedly enhanced in high risk situations. Also, females' altruism was considerably more reduced by increased risk than was altruism in males. In fact, although sex showed a significant main effect, with males more altruistic than females, the effect was due entirely to the marked difference between the sexes in the high risk situations. With low risk, females were more inclined to respond altruistically than were males. These results are consistent with a growing body of social psychological investigation that has emphasized the importance of the interaction between personal and situational factors in affecting social behavior (Bem & Allen, 1974; Ekehammar, 1974; Endler & Hunt, 1968; Mischel, 1973; Price & Bouffard, 1974).

THE TOLL OF FEAR

Most importantly, the present findings support the adaptational nature of social accommodation in the city. In fact, these results underscore the important effect of fear concerning personal safety and vulnerability as an underlying determinant of urban-rural differences in altruism. Risk emerged as the strongest main effect in this study in addition to interacting significantly with sex and the environmental dimension. Risk also underlay the interaction between home town background and urban–rural difference.

Subjects from large city backgrounds were both more altruistic in the city and less fearful for personal safety in the city than were subjects from smaller town backgrounds. A further analysis of the data also revealed an interaction between home town, urban–rural difference, and risk (statistical trend of .052), indicating that the tendency for smaller town subjects to respond less altruistically in the city than subjects from large city backgrounds was due especially to the high risk situations. The fact that subjects from smaller communities were both less altruistic and more fearful in the city than were urbanites suggests the important role of the mass media in shaping attitudes that underlie urban social behavior. In fact, in accord with Gergen's (1973) cogent argument concerning the role of social science in society, we cannot ignore the prospect that highly publicized social psychological findings concerning the unresponsive urbanite have not to some extent reinforced the very phenomena they have studied.

UNDERPLAYING OVERLOAD

Thus, when social accommodation in the city is viewed from an adaptational vantage point, the extent to which people maintain some degree of personal control in the accommodation process becomes particularly evident. Social accommodation emerges as a measured response to perceived environmental constraints, which can be altered as environmental circumstances change. Milgram's (1970) highly publicized discussion of the negative consequences of overload in urban life has reinforced a view of the city dweller as having developed social norms that dictate a generally unresponsive manner in the social sphere. The present findings demonstrate that the urbanite's lack of helpfulness is specific to characteristics of the urban setting and does not reflect an internalized norm of unresponse across all situations. Not only was an unwillingness to help in the city also characteristic of subjects from smaller city backgrounds — who have presumably never suffered the stimulus overload of urban life — but such persons were even less helpful in the city than was the urbanite. While a number of recent studies (Korte, 1975; Sherrod & Downs, 1974;

Weiner, 1976) have demonstrated a clear negative relationship between altruistic behavior and situations of stimulus overload, based on the present findings, we would argue that such effects are limited to the period during and immediately following overload, and are not internalized and broadly generalized as norms of non-responding.

It should be stressed that these results are not a variance with the *findings* of the previous field studies that have reported less altruism in city than town, but with the *interpretation* of those studies that has attributed such results to personal characteristics of the urbanite. In fact, the present findings may help to shed some light on the considerable confusion and contradiction in the findings of previous field studies in this area. Based on the dramatically strong effects of situational variables in this study, it seems probable that what may have appeared as subtle variations in environment, neediness, or personal risk across studies may in fact have produced marked inconsistencies in experimental results.

A NOTE OF CAUTION

Two cautions should be noted in generalizing the present findings. The self-report measure of helping employed here is subject to possible distortions due to social desirability. However, both the agreement of these results with those of field studies reported by Milgram (1970) using similar helping requests and the willingness of subjects from all backgrounds to admit their strong disinclination to lend a helping hand in the city tend to indicate that such distortion was minimal. An additional concern involves the extent to which subjects at this university are representative of students in other parts of the country. This question could be answered empirically, as 20% of the subject sample reported out-of-state home town backgrounds representing all regions of the country. Analyses of variance indicated no differences between in-state and out-of-state subjects on any of the experimental measures.

SUMMARY

Although previous social psychological research has tended to confound personal and situational effects in investigating urban–rural differences in altruism, both the general interpretation of earlier work and popular public stereotype have tended to support an image of urbanites as less helpful, less cooperative, and socially more remote than their country cousins. The purpose of this study was to investigate systematically the relative importance of situational variables, personal variables, and their interactions as determinants of judged appropriateness of altruistic responses along the urban–rural dimension. These findings offer strong evidence that the reported unwillingness of the urbanite to lend a helping hand is more a function of situational factors and of the interaction between situational and personal variables than of person-centered characteristics alone.

All three situational variables examined in this study (urban–rural difference, urgency of request, and personal risk) exerted dramatic effects on subjects' judgments concerning the appropriateness of altruistic responses. Personal variables were less strongly related to altruism. No main effect was found for size of subjects' home town, and, while sex showed a significant effect, the effect was due entirely to markedly less altruistic responses by females in the high risk situations. Among the study's most interesting findings were a number of interactions between the variables examined. Home town background interacted with urban–rural difference, and personal risk interacted with both sex and urban–rural difference. Although the findings do not disagree with the results of other field studies that have indicated less altruism in city than in town, they do not support the interpretation of those studies that has attributed such results to personal characteristics of the urbanite. The present findings demonstrate that the urbanite's lack of helpfulness does not reflect a generalized norm of unresponse, but rather indicates an active accommodation to the realistic constraints of urban life based on a careful weighing of personal risk, neediness, and characteristics of the environment.

REFERENCES

Bem, D. J., & Allen, A. On predicting some of the people some of the time: The search for cross-situational consistencies in behavior. *Psychological Review*, 1974, *81*, 506–520.

Caplan, N., & Nelson, S. D. On being useful: The nature and consequences of psychological research on social problems. *American Psychologist*, 1973, *28*, 199–211.

Clark, R. D., III, & Word, L. E. Why don't by-standers help? Because of ambiguity? *Journal of Personality and Social Psychology*, 1972, *24*, 392–400.

Ekehammar, B. Interactionism in personality from a historical perspective. *Psychological Bulletin*, 1975, *81*, 1026–1028.

Endler, N. S., & Hunt, J. McV. S-R inventories of hostility and comparisons of the proportions of variance from persons, responses and situations for hostility and anxiousness. *Journal of Personality and Social Psychology*, 1968, *9*, 114–123.

Gergen, K. Social psychology as history. *Journal of Personality and Social Psychology*, 1973, *26*, 308–320.

Korte, C. Helpfulness in Dutch society as a function of urbanization and environmental input. *Journal of Personality and Social Psychology*, 1975, *32*, 996–1003.

Latane, B., & Darley, J. M. *The unresponsive by-stander: Why doesn't he help?* New York: Appleton-Century-Crofts, 1970.

Lesk, S., & Zippel, B. Dependency, threat, and helping in a large city. *Journal of Social Psychology*, 1975, *95*, 185–186.

Merrens, M. R. Nonemergency helping behavior in various sized communities. *Journal of Social Psychology*, 1973, *90*, 327–328.

Milgram, S. The experience of living in cities. *Science*, 1970, *167*, 1461–1468.

Mischel, W. Toward a cognitive social learning reconceptualization of personality. *Psychological Review*, 1973, *80*, 252–283.

Morgan, W. C. Situational specificity in altruistic behavior. *Representative Research in Social Psychology*, 1973, *4*, 56–66.

Price, R. H., & Bouffard, D. L. Behavioral appropriateness and situational constraint as dimensions of social behavior. *Journal of Personality and Social Psychology*, 1974, *30*, 579–586.

Scheider, F. W., & Mockus, Z. Failure to find a rural–urban difference in incidence of altruistic behavior. *Psychological Reports*, 1974, *35*, 294.

Sherrod, D. R., & Downs, R. Environmental determinants of altruism: The effects of stimulus overload and perceived control on helping. *Journal of Experimental Social Psychology*, 1974, *10*, 468–479.

Weiner, F. H. Altruism, ambience, and action: The effects of rural and urban rearing on helping behavior. *Journal of Personality and Social Psychology*, 1976, *34*, 112–124.

PART III

ENVIRONMENTAL SCHEMATIZATION

ENVIRONMENTAL SCHEMATIZATION

*W*hat do I see when I notice this bottle [of wine]? The answer would seem very simple. . . . I can go on and enumerate all the details of the bottle. What becomes rapidly clear to me however is that in this way I shall certainly not come nearer to what happened when looking up I saw the bottle standing there. What I saw was very definitely not green glass, white label, lead capsule, etc. What I saw in reality, well, that was something like a disappointment that my friend had not come, the loneliness of my evening (Van Den Berg, 1955).

Concentrate for a moment on the environment where you live. What are your perceptions and feelings? Like the person in the example above, your experience likely includes an image of particular physical objects, superimposed on which is a complexity of personal meanings: An oil painting — a gift from an old friend; a history textbook — a four-week hassle with the bookstore; a wood carving — a souvenir of last summer's trip to Mexico.

Among the most exciting discoveries in my research in the field of environmental psychology has been a realization that the very definition of the physical environment involves an active, complex, and creative human process. For human perception of the physical environment is unlike the objective representations captured through the photographer's lens or the architects's blueprint. To the human perceiver the physical environment is imbued with personal meaning. We will refer to this process of shaping, reconstructing, and organizing the environment into a fabric woven of personal meaning as *environmental schematization*. In this section we will examine in detail this fascinating process through which personal experience restructures the humanly perceived environment.

In environmental coping and social accommodation we have viewed individuals responding to challenging environmental circumstances. Our understanding and interpretation of their responses have been predicated on our *own* vantage point in viewing the antecedent environmental events. In fact, as we will see in this section, a full appreciation of environment–behavior relationships is impossible without comprehending how the environment is viewed by the particular observer. For, in effect, different observers perceive different environments. We will see how the apparently simple act of environmental perception emerges as one of active management and personal creativity.

RESEARCHING SCHEMATIZATION

I decided to investigate the process of environmental schematization in terms of two issues of contemporary interest in psychology. First, I speculated that in accord with psychology's growing interest in sex differences in psychological functioning, it seemed possible that males and females might schematize the environment in somewhat different ways. Second, I postulated that individual differences in environmental schematization related to differential spatial behavior patterns might afford an explanation of the reportedly high "error" rates in cognitive mapping tasks. The two environmental settings selected for the research reported here are especially germane to the experience of university students — a university housing environment and a university campus setting. Again, the studies are methodologically diverse, including a survey study and a design employing both behavioral mapping and cognitive mapping in conjunction.

Chapter 8 describes the results of an environmental survey administered to residents of a university housing environment, which was designed to measure sex-related differences in environmental schematization. We will see that dramatic differences exist in the ways men and women schematize the environment. Women, for example, view the environment in relatively stronger personal terms than do men. Also, while for men the environment is seen in a somewhat more asocial manner, for women the environment is viewed as more social.

Chapter 9 presents a study of university students, where behavioral and cognitive methodologies are employed simultaneously to investigate the relationship between environmental behavior and cognitive mapping. We will discover that even the physical maps that people draw of the environment reflect a complex and active human process. For different individuals' maps differ in subtle ways according to corresponding differences in the manners in which those persons behave in the settings being mapped. Some environmental psychologists have reported feeling perplexed about the considerable degree of error apparent in people's environmental maps. We will see that what at first appear as errors, are, in fact, quite understandable individual reconstructions of the physical environment to accord with personal activity patterns in the environment.

DYNAMIC FEATURES OF ENVIRONMENTAL SCHEMATIZATION

Before turning to the two research studies in this section, it will be helpful to identify some basic features of environmental schematization, which should be emphasized in reading the case examples. The dynamic aspect of environmental schematization is reflected in two ways: (1) environmental schematization is an inherently active process, and (2) the process is highly personalized.

Active

The process of perceiving the physical environment may initially appear straightforward and rather passive. We will discover, however, that environmental schematization represents a vitally active and surprisingly complex process. For people do not passively record the environment. Rather in environmental schematization we see the individual actively imposing on the physical setting a complex array of feelings, attitudes, and meanings. In fact, as Bronfenbrenner (1976) has noted in referring to the observation of Mead (1934), it is essentially in the human capacity to attribute meaning to stimuli that we differ most from other species. We will find, for example, that men and women differ dramatically in the ways in which they impose personal and social meanings on their experience of the environment. In addition, we will discover that in the cognitive mapping task the objective or "Euclidian" environment is restructured and altered by individuals in consistent and understandable ways.

Personal

Although our everyday social interchange rests on an assumption of a consensually validated environment, we will see in this section that in considerable detail environmental perception is a personal, unique, and idiosyncratic experience! For different people see different environments — environments that vary systematically as a function of the richly unique variations between people in personal experiences, attitudes, and needs. Sex-related differences in environmental schematization are a product of the differential attitudes, sensitivities, and social needs, which derive from the unique "life spaces" or psychological environments of men and women. In addition we will find that supposed "errors" in cognitive mapping, in fact, bear a clear relationship to individual differences in personal environmental activity patterns.

REFERENCES

Bronfenbrenner, U. The experimental ecology of education. *Educational Researcher*, 1976, 5, 5–15.
Mead, G. H. *Mind, self, and society*. Chicago: University of Chicago Press, 1934.
Van Den Berg, J. H. *The phenomenological approach to psychiatry*. Springfield, Illinois: Thomas, 1955.

CHAPTER 8

Sex Differences in Schematizing the Behavioral Environment*

On a winter evening amidst a driving snowstorm a man on horseback arrived at an inn, happy to have reached a shelter after hours of riding over the wind-swept plain on which the blanket of snow had covered all paths and landmarks. The landlord who came to the door viewed the stranger with surprise and asked him whence he came. The man pointed in the direction straight away from the inn, whereupon the landlord, in a tone of awe and wonder, said: "Do you know that you have ridden across the Lake of Constance?" At which the rider dropped stone dead at his feet (Koffka, 1935).

Koffka recounts this old German legend to emphasize dramatically the fundamental difference between the "geographic" and the "behavioral" environment. While geographic environment refers to the objective geophysical environment, the behavioral environment is the environment as uniquely perceived by a particular individual. Though the emerging discipline of environmental psychology (Craik, 1970; Proshansky, Ittelson, & Rivlin, 1970; Wohlwill, 1970) has generated a renewed psychological interest in the molar physical environment, little attention has been addressed to the behavioral or phenomenological environment.

*The research discussed in this chapter was conducted in collaboration with Carole K. Holahan.

The concept of behavioral environment is particularly relevant to psychology's growing concern with sex-related differences across a range of psychological processes and functions. A small body of theoretical speculation, with little empirical support to date, has focused on the issue of basic differences in the ways males and females see, understand, and communicate about the physical environment.

Gutmann (1965) has addressed this issue in terms of developmental differences in style of ego functioning. He stresses that the ego is adaptationally "fitted" to environmental demands, and that contrasting environmental pressures for males and females lead to correspondingly unique styles of ego functioning. Gutmann's analysis is based on and specific to the life-style patterns characteristic of the traditional male and female roles within our culture. The typical business and professional milieu of the male may be described as *allocentric*; it is impersonal and is not ordered from oneself. The female's typical domestic milieu can be described, in contrast, as *autocentric;* it is highly personalized and represents "an extension of the homemaker's persona." According to Gutmann, these basic differences also color schematization in the social realm. In the allocentric milieu, other persons are objectified, while in the autocentric milieu, the distinction between self and others is blurred by the relatedness of individuals in the groupings of family and neighborhood.

Sex-related differences in relating to the social environment have been further examined by Bakan (1966). He employs the label *agency* to describe the male's characteristic individualistic, agressive, and self-protective style, and *communion* to refer to the female's characteristic orientation toward interpersonal contact, cooperation, and group belongingness. Typical, in addition, of the agentic style is a repression and control of affect, while the communal orientation fosters an open and free expression of feelings. Block (1973) has applied these concepts in a critical and integrative analysis of a wide range of culturally diverse research dealing with sex-related differences in the instrumental and expressive domains of socialization.

Carlson (1971) has attempted to lend empirical support to the concepts of both Gutmann and Bakan. While she has examined sex differences in representations of self, others, and the future, in addition to the physical environment, our concern is limited to Carlson's investigation in the latter realm. Based primarily on Gutmann, she proposed that females would represent the physical environment in relatively more self-centered terms than would males. To subjects' written descriptions of the physical–geographic environment where they lived longest during their first 10 years, she applied a dichotomous measure differentiating between personalized versus objective accounts. Her results demonstrated that twice as many females as males responded with personalized environmental descriptions.

Summarizing this previous work, two propositions may be advanced concerning specific psychological dimensions along which males and females differ in their schematizations of the physical environment. First, based on Gutmann and the empirical evidence of Carlson, males are more likely to describe the physical environment in objective terms, while females view the environment in more personalized ways. Second, according to both Gutmann and Bakan, males are expected to describe the environment in terms of an individualistic orientation, and females in a more social vein.

A STUDY OF ENVIRONMENTAL SCHEMATIZATION

The purpose of the present study was to investigate further at an empirical level differences between males and females in their schematization of the behavioral environment. Specific study goals included: (1) replication of Carlson's findings concerning the personalization dimension using a more precisely defined quantitative measurement scale; (2) examination, in addition, of sex differences in environmental descriptions along the social dimension; (3) an extension of the analysis to include sex-related differences in the schematization of a contemporaneous environment in addition to the childhood home setting. Subjects in the study were 100 introductory pyschology students who fulfilled a course requirement by participating. The sample included 50 males and 50 females, who were tested in three mixed-sex groups.

MEASURES OF SCHEMATIZATION

Instructions for the setting descriptions were as follows: (1) Describe below the environment where you are presently living at college. (2) Describe below the environment where you lived longest during your first 10 years.

Each setting description was scored along two pyschological dimensions: Personalization and Social Emphasis. The Personalization score indicated the extent to which the description reflected a personalized or subjective orientation in contrast to an objective one, and was based on references to personal activities, attitudes, or values. The Social Emphasis score indicated the extent to which the description reflected a social or group orientation in contrast to an individualistic one, and was based on references to other persons, interpersonal concerns, or friendship. The score for each dimension ranged from 1 (no expression) to 5 (extensive expression). The scoring criteria for the two dimensions are as follows:

Degree of Personalization

1 point	Impersonal, objectified perspective
2 points	Reference to idiosyncratic objects in the environment
3 points	Reference to personal activities or behavior
4 points	Reference to personal attitudes, values, or opinions
5 points	Extensive dwelling on personal attitudes, values, or opinions

Degree of Social Emphasis

1 point	Asocial, individualistic orientation
2 points	Reference to other persons
3 points	Reference to friends or friendships
4 points	Reference to intimacy in friendship, e.g., closeness, neediness, human warmth
5 points	Extensive dwelling on intimacy in friendship

Scoring was conducted by two independent raters, who were blind to both the study's hypotheses and the sex of the subject. Interrater reliability exceeded 90% on both measures. The zero-order correlation between the two dimensions was .51.

SEX DIFFERENCES IN PERSONALIZATION

Childhood Environment

Males and females differed markedly in the degree of personalization reflected in their description of their childhood home environments. For this description, females showed a mean personalization score of 3.26, in contrast to only 2.70 for male respondents. This difference between the two sexes was statistically significant by the analyses of variance ($F = 6.98$, $df = 1/98$, $p < .01$). The qualitative character of responses by the two sexes also differed dramatically. For example, one male student responded: "I lived in a three-bedroomed house in Oak Cliff, a suburb of Dallas. It was in a basically white middle class neighborhood." In sharp contrast, a female subject reported: "My home was a place of hustle and bustle. A thousand things were going on at one time. There was never a dull moment. Our family did lots of things together as we were all very sports-minded. We helped and encouraged one another in anything which was done."

Present Environment

On the description of the present environment, females were again significantly higher in their level of personalization than were male respondents ($F = 15.47$, $df = 1/98$, $p < .001$). The mean personalization score for females on the present environment description was 3.32, compared with 2.52 for males. Again, the responses for the two sexes were qualitatively quite different. For example, a male subject stated: "Small, one-bedroom, furnished apartment, off-campus, i.e., 'efficiency,' with kitchen, the usual furniture, high rent and utilities, roaches, and no view." In comparison, a female student responded: "I'm living in an apartment on Lakeshore with my sister, her best friend, and my best friend. We have a cat and lots of mostly dead plants! The apartment is colorful, with lots of posters of places we'd like to visit. We try to keep it pretty clean. I'm planning on getting married, so it's got lots of stuff lying around."

SEX DIFFERENCES IN SOCIAL EMPHASIS

Childhood Environment

A sharp difference between male and female respondents emerged on the social emphasis dimension of the childhood home environment description. On this description, the female sample demonstrated a mean social emphasis score of 2.76, and the male sample a score of 2.34. This difference between the two sexes showed a strong statistical trend by the analysis of variance ($F = 3.32$, $df = 1/98$, $p < .08$). The qualitative difference between the descriptions of males and females was particularly revealing. One male student, for example, wrote: "California coast (San Diego), small suburb, large house in hills." A female respondent, in contrast, stated: "I am the oldest of five children, three boys and two girls. Family life is something I love. As a family we were, and still are, very close. Since I was the oldest, I always had to make sure nothing went wrong, or else I'd be blamed. I feel that the environment I came from was warm, loving, friendly, and respecting."

Present Environment

Males and females, again, differed dramatically in the level of social emphasis revealed in the present environment description. In describing the present environment, females showed a mean social emphasis score of 2.96, as opposed to only 2.12 for male subjects. This difference between the two sexes was statistically significant by the analysis of variance ($F = 18.55$, $df = 1/98$, $p < .001$). Again, a noteworthy qualitative contrast between the descriptions of males and females was apparent. For example, a male subject replied: "In an apartment, which is the upstairs of an old house. It's small. It has one bedroom, kitchen, living area, bath, run down." A female student, in comparison, wrote: "I live in an apartment with two other girls. We get along very well, our personalities are compatible, and we enjoy each others' company. My old roommate and I did not get along well. Living with Jan and Lecia is a very pleasant break from Kathy. All in all, we get along great — it makes for a very happy environment."

SOME SPECULATION ON SEX DIFFERENCES IN ENVIRONMENTAL SCHEMATIZATION

The findings from this study afford strong evidence that males and females differ dramatically in the manner in which they schematize the behavioral environment. While women tend to view the world in markedly personal and social terms, men are inclined to see the environment in a relatively impersonal and asocial manner. These differences between the two sexes in viewing the environment pertain to both childhood and contemporaneous environmental settings.

The present results are congruent with Gutmann's (1965) notion of the male's typical *allocentric* or impersonal style of viewing the world, in contrast to the female's *autocentric* or personalized manner of relating to the environment. These findings are also consistent with Bakan's (1966) view of the *agentic* or oppositional mode of approaching the social environment characteristics of males, as compared with the female's *communal* or cooperative stance toward the social milieu. In addition, the present study supports and extends Carlson's (1971) earlier empirical investigation of sex differences in the degree of personalization involved in descriptions of the childhood home environment.

The differing styles in which men and women schematize the behavioral environment are probably a function of a number of influences. Further investigation in this area will be essential to identifying and examining some of the factors that underlie sex differences in environmental schematization. For example, the present findings most likely reflect the cumulative influences of both contrasting societal sex roles and differences in personality characteristically associated with the two sexes. The effects of these two factors might be examined separately through including measures of psychological masculinity and femininity and an index of traditionality versus innovation in sex role conception. A related issue concerns the extent to which differing environmental descriptions between males and females may reflect actual differences in environment as well as differentially valent perceptions of the environment. Here, a measure might be included to reflect sex differences in describing the *same* environmental setting, such as a small coeducational dormitory or a cooperative apartment setting. Finally, generalization of the present findings will necessitate research with a diversified subject sample in addition to university students. In fact, broader sampling will allow investigation of a number of additional questions, such as the possible interaction of sex differences with variables such as age, life-style, and occupational choice in affecting environmental schematization.

SUMMARY

The results of this study supported the proposition that there are systematic differences in the ways in which males and females schematize their behavioral environments. While males were inclined to see the environment in relatively objective and nonsocial terms, females tended to view the environment in a more personalized and social manner. These results were consistent with expectations based on the theoretical views of both Gutmann (1965) and Bakan (1966). Koffka's (1935) emphasis on psychological investigation of the behavioral environment was based on a conviction that until psychology is able to comprehend the environment as it is seen by the individual, accurate behavioral prediction will be impossible. The present findings underscore the need for further investigation of the behavioral environment in psychological research concerned with sex-related differences in functioning. If the behavioral environments in which males and females develop, explore, cope, and learn differ systematically, psychological understanding of a range of other differences in functioning between the sexes may be predicted upon a more complete comprehension of the different worlds of males and females.

REFERENCES

Bakan, D. *The duality of human existence.* Chicago: Rand McNally, 1966.

Block, J. H. Conceptions of sex role: Some cross-cultural and longitudinal perspectives. *American Psychologist*, 1973, *28*, 512–527.

Carlson, R. Sex differences in ego functioning. *Journal of Consulting and Clinical Psychology*, 1971, *37*, 267–277.

Craik, K. H. Environmental psychology. In K. H. Craik, B. Kleinmuntz, R. Roshow, R. Rosenthal, J. A. Cheyne, & R. H. Walters (Eds.), *New directions in psychology* (Vol. 4). New York: Holt, Rinehart & Winston, 1970.

Gutmann, D. Women and the conception of ego strength. *Merrill-Palmer Quarterly*, 1965, *11*, 229–240.

Koffka, K. *Principles of Gestalt psychology.* New York: Harcourt, Brace and World, 1935.

Proshansky, H. M., Ittelson, W. H., & Rivlin, L. G. *Environmental psychology: Man and his physical setting.* New York: Holt, Rinehart & Winston, 1970.

Wohlwill, J. The emerging discipline of environmental psychology. *American Psychologist*, 1970, *25*, 303–312.

CHAPTER 9

Errors in Cognitive Mapping: A Behavioral Interpretation*

An especially exciting area of investigation in the field of environment and behavior that reflects the active role people play in evolving schemata of the physical environment has come to be called cognitive mapping. Cognitive maps, alternatively referred to as mental maps or environmental images, refer to people's cognitive representations of the spatial environment. *Cognitive mapping* has referred to the process of acquisition, amalgamation, and storage of these cognitive representations (Downs & Stea, 1973). As mentioned earlier, the seminal work in this area was conducted by Lynch (1960), who collected cognitive maps of Boston, Jersey City, and Los Angeles. Some later studies followed Lynch's lead and gathered cognitive maps of a number of cities throughout the world — Amsterdam, Rotterdam, and The Hague (de Jonge, 1962), Chicago (Saarinen, 1969), Ciudad Guayana (Appleyard, 1969, 1970), Milan and Rome (Francescato & Mebane, 1973). Though cognitive maps can be generated through a range of verbal or graphic mediums, the predominant technique has been through map drawing as established by Lynch (Stea & Downs, 1970).

Research on cognitive mapping has been almost exclusively descriptive rather than explicative. While we know *what* is

*The research discussed in this chapter was conducted in collaboration with Mirilia Bonnes Dobrowolny.

mapped, we know very little about *how* cognitive maps are generated or altered (Downs & Stea, 1973). For example, we have learned that the veridicality of cognitive maps is typically low, with such maps offering poor representations of the actual environment (Appleyard, 1973). Downs and Stea have defined distortions in cognitive maps as "cognitive transformations of both distance and direction, such that an individual's subjective geometry deviates from the Euclidean view of the world." Yet, we do not know how or why such individual distortions in mapping develop. While Downs and Stea have suggested that individual differences in cognitive mapping may be a function of variations in spatial activity patterns, their opinion is based on speculation; as no previous research has examined this issue empirically.

DESIGNING AN INTERACTIONAL STUDY

The purpose of the present study was to investigate how distortions in cognitive mapping are caused, by comparing cognitive maps of a given environment with spatial behavior patterns in that setting. We hoped that the nature of the activity patterns in the particular setting would tell us something of how the cognitive map of that setting is formed. In effect, the study employs cognitive mapping and behavioral mapping strategies in conjunction, using the behavioral data to lend both credence and elucidation to the cognitive mapping findings.

The rationale of this study was to select a number of cognitive and behavioral measures, which have been examined in previous work, and to collect and compare both types of data in the same environmental setting. The cognitive variables examined included *emphasis* in mapping, e.g., map borders and spatial features included in the map, and *distortions* in mapping, e.g., size exaggerations of spatial features or dislocations of the center of the spatial area. The behavioral measures collected involved behavioral observations of *collective* activity patterns of all persons in selected parts of the setting and self-reports from individuals of *personal* behavior patterns in the area. We chose a university campus

environment for the study because the physical size of the campus
seemed ideal for the research objectives. While the campus was
small enough to allow coherent maps, it was large and complex
enough to elicit significant distortions or errors. Two hypotheses
were advanced: (a) borders and spatial features included in the cognitive maps would be directly related to personal and collective
behavior in the environment, and (b) size exaggeration of spatial
features in cognitive maps and dislocations of the campus center
would be directly related to individual differences in personal
behavior in the environment.

Cognitive maps of the university campus were collected from
all 105 students enrolled in a course in community psychology at
the University of Texas. This class was selected because it reflected
a representative cross-section of the overall student population,
with students broadly distributed across year levels and major areas
of study and balanced across sex. The cognitive maps were scored in
three ways. First, spatial zones were determined which reflected
areas of spatial emphases based on two types of independent information — map borders and frequency of occurrence of identifiable
spatial features in the maps. In addition, a size exaggeration score
was determined for each of the four chief outdoor malls on the
campus. Finally, a centrifugal distortion score was calculated, which
indicated the degree to which the center of a subject's map deviated
from the true center of the campus. Each of these cognitive map
measures was compared in turn with measures of environmental
behavior. Personal behavior was assessed by asking subjects to
indicate on their maps where they would go on campus to engage in
each of a number of specific types of behavior. The Personal
Behavior measure allowed indications of both average group
activity in the setting and of individual differences in spatial
behavior. Collective behavior was determined by behavioral
observations of outdoor behavior patterns on the university
campus. The Collective Behavior measure permitted an index of
average activity patterns across a large number of campus users, in
addition to an objective check on the self-reported personal
behavior. Three specific subcategories of behavior were
investigated under both Personal and Collective Behavior: (1) Fre-

quency of Use, (2) Sitting, and (3) Socializing. These behavior sub-categories were chosen because we felt they reflected some degree of behavioral importance associated with the spatial area. It was assumed that the first two behaviors related to familiarity with and preference for the area, while the third behavior related to social meaning or investment in the area.

MAPPING AND BEHAVIORAL MEASURES

Cognitive Maps

The cognitive maps were collected in a group format during a regularly scheduled class period. The experimenter provided each subject with one piece of 8¼" x 11" white unlined paper and a pencil, and read the following instructions.

> I'd like you to draw a map of the University of Texas campus on the paper I've handed out. Imagine that the purpose of the map is for another student, who is new to the campus, as a guide to orienting himself and finding his way about on the campus. Let's allow a maximum of 20 minutes for completing the map. I have a few questions to ask after everyone has finished the map, so if you finish before 20 minutes, would you wait until the others are done.

The scoring of the cognitive maps was performed by two under-graduates, who were trained in using the scoring procedures during seven hours of practice scoring on pilot map data. The scorers were blind both to the study's hypotheses and to the behavioral mapping findings. Interrater reliability between the two scorers exceeded 90% on all measures.

Personal Behavior

After the 20 minutes had elapsed, the measure of personal behavior was collected in the following way. The experimenter stated:

> Now I have a few short questions. Please don't change any details on the maps as you answer these questions.
>   1. Where do you most prefer to go outdoors on campus to sit and relax alone? Put a #1 in that place on the map.

2. Where do you most prefer to go outdoors on campus to talk with a friend? Put a #2 in that place.

3. Where would you prefer to go outdoors on campus to hand out pamphlets to the largest number of people? Put a #3 in that place.

4. At what point do you typically enter the campus? Put an arrow in that place.

Each of the first three questions corresponded to the behavior subcategories, Sitting, Socializing, and Frequency, respectively.

Collective Behavior

Collective behavior was measured through behavioral observations outdoors on the university campus during a one-month period following the collection of the self-report measures. The behavioral technique employed was an adaptation of the behavioral mapping procedure developed by Ittelson, Rivlin, and Proshansky (1970). The behavioral map consisted of a record of the number of individuals engaged in each of three predetermined behavior subcategories in each subarea observed in the campus environment. The behavior subcategories that were recorded were defined as follows: (1) Frequency — the total number of individuals observed in a given area; (2) Sitting — the number of individuals sitting (or lying) in a given area; and (3) Socializing — the number of individuals involved in clear social groupings of two or more persons in a given setting. Observations involved complete coverage of all physical spaces in the selected subareas on a time-sampling basis. Observations were recorded on data sheets designed for quick and easy use by observers. Previous research has shown the behavioral mapping procedure to have high inter-observer and split-half reliability (Ittelson, Rivlin, & Proshansky, 1970). After training in the specific behavioral scoring procedures used here, interrater reliability was determined for the two observers. Agreement exceeded 90% on all measures.

The behavioral observations were conducted in sunny weather where the temperature ranged from 65 to 75°. All observations were performed between 10:00 a.m. and 12:00 a.m. on Monday, Wednesday, and Friday. Observations were carried out while classes were in session because pilot data had indicated that reliable measurement was impossible during the excessively heavy flow between classes, and that the relative distributions of behavior types over the setting correlated highly between the class-in-session and class-out-of-session periods. For observational purposes, the campus was divided into 190 continuous grid spaces, and 10% of these spaces were randomly selected for observation. The four campus malls were observed in toto. Each observation site was observed on a total of four different days. Two observers were employed, who worked independently and were counterbalanced over the observational sites.

SCORING THE COGNITIVE MAPS

Spatial Zones Based on Map Borders

The boundary feature at the four compass quadrants was ascertained from each map, and a modal boundary across subjects was determined at each quadrant. A clear pattern of group consensus concerning map boundaries emerged, with campus streets the modal feature at each quadrant. The western boundary was agreed on by 100 subjects and was the clearest map boundary. The street selected reflects a sharp break on the actual campus between the campus and the surrounding community. It is referred to colloquially as "the Drag" and is populated by heavily frequented lunch spots and diversified commercial establishments. The southern and northern boundaries on the cognitive maps reflected diminutions in the size of the actual university campus. Seventy-two subjects agreed on the southern boundary, and 60 subjects on the boundary on the north. Both streets selected as the north and south boundaries are active traffic arteries through the campus. The eastern boundary reflected a less clear consensus, with 46 subjects selecting one street as a boundary and 40 subjects choosing an alternative street. Again both streets are major traffic routes, and both represent significant diminutions in the actual size of the campus. Based on these border selections, it is possible to identify three distinct border zones, in the cognitive maps. Border zone 1 is

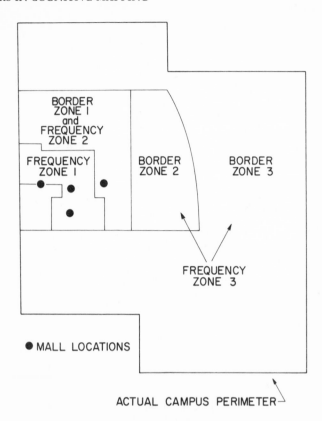

Figure 5. Schematic representation of border zones and frequency zones relative to the actual university campus.

the bounded area mapped by the largest number of subjects, while border zone 2 is the area mapped by the second largest number of subjects. Border zone 3 is the space on the actual campus that was excluded by almost all subjects in the mapping exercise. This finding is especially noteworthy as zone 3 was totally excluded on almost all cognitive maps even though it represented the largest physical area of the three zones on the actual campus.

Spatial Zones Based on Frequency of Spatial Features

A frequency distribution was determined reflecting the total number of times each building on the campus appeared across the maps of all subjects. All buildings that occurred on at least 50% of subjects' maps were identified and labeled on a map of the campus. In addition, those buildings that occurred on at least 90% of subjects' maps were labeled on the campus map. A clear pattern of emphasis again emerged, reflecting three frequency zones, which corresponded in part with the border zones. Frequency zone 1 marks the spatial area that included 9 of the 10 buildings occurring on 90% of subject's maps. This zone included the South Mall, the Main Mall, and the northern half of the West Mall. All of these spaces were also included within border zone 1. Frequency zone 2 consisted of the spatial area that included almost all of the buildings occurring on 50% of subjects' maps. This zone corresponded with the remaining space in border zone 1. Frequency zone 3 marked the area where few buildings occurred on 50% of subjects maps, and was a very large area that included both border zone 2 and 3. Figure 5 depicts schematically the border zones and frequency zones relative to the full size of the actual university campus.

RELATING CAMPUS BEHAVIOR TO THE MAP ZONES

Collective Behavior

Outdoor behavior observed on the campus for each of the behavior subcategories — i.e., Frequency, Sitting, Socializing — was sorted in terms of the border zones and the frequency zones established from the cognitive maps. The behavior score for each zone was based on behavior per standard area, with the standard area defined as the size of one of the 190 spatial units used for conducting the outdoor observations.

A chi-square analysis was performed on each behavior category within each of the two spatial breakdowns, i.e., border zones and frequency zones. The expected frequency for the analysis was determined on the assumption that by chance behavior would be distributed equally across the spatial zones. Table 10 summarizes the spatial breakdown of collective behavior, along with the results of the chi-square analyses. As predicted, there was a statistically significant relationship between map emphases, as

Table 10. Collective Behavior Distributed across
Spatial Zones

Behavior type	1	2	3	Total	df	χ^2
Border zones						
Frequency	105.7	67.6	12.4	185.7	2	71.09[a]
Sitting	22.8	10.8	4.4	38.0	2	14.02[a]
Socializing	31.6	16.8	5.4	53.8	2	19.25[a]
Frequency zones						
Frequency	314.8	83.2	23.4	421.4	2	337.27[a]
Sitting	134.9	11.4	5.7	152.0	2	210.36[a]
Socializing	76.4	26.6	7.7	110.7	2	68.27[a]

[a]$p < .001$.

reflected in the selection of both borders and spatial features, and each of the three subcategories of collective behavior.

Personal Behavior

Subjects' self-report responses of their typical outdoor campus behavior for each behavior subcategory was sorted into the border zones and frequency zones. A chi-square analysis was again performed on each behavior subcategory within each of the two spatial breakdowns. The expected frequency for the analysis was again determined on the assumption that by chance behavior would be distributed equally across the physical space of the campus. Table 11 summarizes the spatial breakdown of personal behavior, along with the results of the chi-square analyses. There was again, as anticipated, a statistically significant relationship between both border selection and spatial feature frequency and each of the three subcategories of Personal Behavior. In addition, it should be noted that the Personal Behavior responses were in close agreement with the Collective Behavior data, indicating that self-reported behavior corresponded closely with actual activity patterns on campus.

Table 11. Personal Behavior Distributed across Spatial
Zones

Behavior type	1	2	3	Total[a]	df	χ^2
Border zones						
Frequency	97	2	3	102	2	175.07[b]
Sitting	87	6	6	99	2	132.54[b]
Socializing	92	2	3	97	2	165.18[b]
Frequency zones						
Frequency	87	10	5	102	2	131.34[b]
Sitting	55	32	12	99	2	28.05[b]
Socializing	58	34	5	97	2	43.55[b]

[a] Subject totals reflect the failure of some subjects to respond to the respective item.
[b] $p < .001$.

PERSONAL BEHAVIOR AND COGNITIVE DISTORTIONS

Size Exaggeration

Size Exaggeration referred to an augmentation in the size of a spatial area on a cognitive map beyond the size of the corresponding space on the actual campus. Size Exaggeration scores were calculated for each subject for the four campus malls using the following procedure. The Size Exaggeration score was defined as the difference between the percent of space a given mall occupied on the actual campus and the percent of space the same mall occupied on a subject's cognitive map. The spatial size of each mall on the cognitive maps was operationally defined as the rectangle enclosed by the clearly identifiable buildings on the maps which bordered that mall on the actual campus. The corresponding size of the mall on the actual campus was measured in the same manner. The highest Size Exaggeration score occurred for the

South Mall (2.48), followed by the West Mall (1.55), the Main Mall (1.11), and finally the East Mall (.74). These differences between malls were statistically significant beyond the .001 level ($F = 28.69$, $df = 3/309$).

The relationship between Size Exaggeration and Personal Behavior was examined in the following manner. For each campus mall, the Size Exaggeration score for subjects who reported using that mall for at least one subcategory of personal behavior was compared with the corresponding score for subjects who showed no personal behavior for the same mall. (The East Mall, where only 6 subjects reported using the mall at all was not examined in this way.) Table 12 shows the relationship between Size Exaggeration and personal use for the West, South, and Main Malls, along with the results of the corresponding t tests. The predicted significant relationship between mall use and degree of spatial exaggeration was found for the South and Main Malls. While the mean difference was in the expected direction for the West Mall, the difference was not statistically significant.

Centrifugal Distortion

Centrifugal Distortion referred to a displacement of the campus center on a cognitive map away from the campus's true center.

Table 12. Size Exaggeration Scores by Personal Use for Three Campus Malls

Mall	Personal behavior					
	Use	N	Do not use	N	df^a	t
West	1.78	55	1.64	40	93	.54
South	3.11	63	1.78	37	98	3.02^b
Main	1.78	40	1.10	51	89	2.06^c

[a]dfs reflect the failure of some subjects to map the respective mall.
[b]$p < .005$ (directional test).
[c]$p < .05$ (directional test).

Centrifugal Distortion scores were calculated for each subject using the following procedure. The physical center of each cognitive map was determined, and the corresponding point on the objective map of the campus was marked. The centers for both the cognitive maps and the actual campus were operationally fixed by drawing a rectangle enclosing all drawn campus features and setting the center at the cross point of the two diagonals. The radius was then drawn on the objective map from the true center through the subject's subjective center to the campus's outer boundary. The Centrifugal Distortion score was defined as the percent of deviation of the subjective center along the radius away from the true center.

The relationship between Centrifugal Distortion and Personal Behavior was examined in the following manner. The Centrifugal Distortion score for subjects who reported their typical entry point toward the periphery of the actual campus was compared with the corresponding score for subjects who indicated their typical entry point was closer to the center of the actual campus. The difference between peripheral and central entry was based primarily on the campus bus stop frequented by commuters and the dormitory location for on-campus residents. For peripheral entry subjects the Centrifugal Distortion score was 60.46, compared to 48.64 for central entry subjects. This difference is in the predicted direction and is statistically significant with the t test at the .005 level (t = 3.09, df = 100, directional test).

REINTERPRETING MAPPING ERRORS

The chief contribution of this study in terms of the cognitive mapping process is that the conjoint use of the behavioral approach offers explicative data in an area of investigation that traditionally has been almost exclusively descriptive. The present findings shed some clarifying light on Appleyard's (1973) position that the veridicality of cognitive maps is noticeably low. While the data indicate marked discrepancies between cognitive maps and the actual campus setting, they demonstrate further that such distortions, rather than reflecting random error, bear a consistent and interpretable relationship to patterns of environmental behavior. This relationship was evident for a range of apparent "errors" in mapping, including distortion in map borders, exclusion of spatial features, size discrepancies, and displacement of the campus center.

IMPLICATIONS FOR URBAN MAPPING

The present study represents only a first step in a potentially broad sphere of inquiry. The generality of impact and broader ecological relevance of these findings will necessitate an extension of this type of research design from the campus to the urban environment and from circumscribed categories of behavior to the broad realm of urban life-style. For example, these findings bear some implications for research involving cognitive mapping of the urban environment in the tradition of Lynch (1960) by underscoring the potential value of integrating cognitive and behavioral strategies within single research paradigms. A behavioral orientation may help to elucidate some of the recently observed group variations in mapping the urban environment. Appleyard (1970) found differences in cognitive maps of Ciudad Guayana related to educational level, with the maps of less educated groups tending to more heavily reflect subjective experience and those of more educated groups portraying the city more objectively. Francescato and Mebane (1973) reported differences in cognitive maps of both Milan and Rome between middle and lower classes, younger and older residents, and natives and nonnatives. Research approaches employing both cognitive and behavioral measures could tell us precisely what types of behavioral variations are related to specific differences in residents' maps of their urban environment.

One fruitful direction for such research may be investigation of the relationship between contrasting urban life-styles and variations in cognitive maps. Michelson (1970) and Michelson and Reed (1970) have proposed a framework for conceptualizing urban life-styles that might prove valuable to investigators concerned with relating environmental behavior to cognitive mapping. Milgram (1974) has, for example, afforded some initial thoughts on the relationship between life-style and the mapping of urban settings in his research of the Paris environment. An imperative initial step to such integration is increased communication between the cognitive and behavioral camps in terms of conceptual issues, design strategies, and a common research language. Only then will the possibility exist for research programs incorporating both cognitive and behavioral emphases as converging measures of the complex problems posed by the urban environment.

SUMMARY

The purpose of this study was to investigate how distortions in cognitive mapping are caused, by comparing cognitive maps of a given environment with spatial behavior patterns in that setting. We predicted that both observed and reported behavior patterns in the environment would be directly related to those spatial areas that were emphasized or excluded in cognitive maps and to sub-jective distortions in mapping. The study's findings provided strong support for the proposed hypotheses. We had predicted that map borders and spatial features included in cognitive maps would be directly related to patterns of personal and collective behavior in the campus environment. The border zones and frequency zones established from the cognitive maps were in fact significantly related to all three of the behavior subcategories — i.e., frequency, sitting, and socializing — under both personal and collective behavior. We had further proposed that a direct relationship would exist between patterns of personal behavior in the environment and both size exaggeration of spatial features and displacement of the campus center in the cognitive maps. As predicted, a significant direct relationship was found between both the degree of size exaggeration of campus malls and the tendency to distort the true center of the campus and personal use patterns in the campus setting. Most important in terms of the dynamic perspective is the finding that what at first appeared as errors in the cognitive maps emerged, in fact, as understandable individual reconstructions of the physical environment to accord with personal environmental activity patterns.

REFERENCES

Appleyard, D. Why buildings are known. *Environment and Behavior*, 1969, *1*, 131–156.
Appleyard, D. Styles and methods of structuring a city. *Environment and Behavior*, 1970, *2*, 100–118.
Appleyard, D. Notes on urban perception and knowledge. In R. M. Downs & D. Stea (Eds.), *Image and environment*. Chicago: Aldine, 1973.
Bechtel, R. B. Human movement and architecture. In H. M. Proshansky, W. H. Ittelson, & L. G. Rivlin (Eds.), *Environmental psychology: Man and his physical setting*. New York: Holt, Rinehart & Winston, 1970.
Brower, S., & Williamson, P. Outdoor recreation as a function of the urban housing environment. *Environment and Behavior*, 1974, *3*, 294–345.
de Jonge, D. Images of urban areas, their structures and psychological foundations. *Journal of the American Institute of Planners*, 1962, *28*, 266–276.
Downs, R. M., & Stea, D. Cognitive maps and spatial behavior: Process and products. In R. M. Downs & D. Stea (Eds.), *Image and environment*. Chicago: Aldine, 1973.
Francescato, D., & Mebane, W. How citizens view two great cities: Milan and Rome. In R. M. Downs & D. Stea (Eds,), *Image and environment*. Chicago: Aldine, 1973.
Holahan, C. J. Environmental effects on outdoor social behavior in a low-income urban neighborhood: A naturalistic investigation. *Journal of Applied Social Psychology*, 1976, *6*, 48–63.
Holahan, C. J., & Saegert, S. Behavioral and attitudinal effects of large scale variation in the physical environment of psychiatric wards. *Journal of Abnormal Psychology*, 1973, *3*, 454–462.
Ittelson, W. H., Proshansky, H. M., & Rivlin, L. G. The environmental psychology of the psychiatric ward. In H. M. Proshansky, W. H. Ittelson, & L. G. Rivlin (Eds.), *Environmental psychology: Man and his physical setting*. New York: Holt, Rinehart & Winston, 1970.
Ittelson, W. H., Rivlin, L. G., & Proshansky, H. M. The use of behavioral maps in environmental psychology. In H. M. Proshansky, W. H. Ittelson, & L. G. Rivlin (Eds.), *Environmental psychology: Man and his physical setting*. New York: Holt, Rinehart & Winston, 1970.
Lynch, K. *The image of the city*. Cambridge, Massachusetts: M.I.T. Press, 1960.
Michelson, W. *Man and his urban environment: A sociological approach*. Reading, Massachusetts: Addison-Wesley, 1970.

Michelson, W., & Reed, P. *The theoretical status and operational usage of life style in environmental research.* Paper presented to the Annual Meeting of the American Sociological Association, Washington, D.C., 1970.

Milgram, S. *Cognitive mapping in Paris and New York.* Paper presented at 82nd Annual Convention of the American Psychological Association, New Orleans, 1974.

Saarinen, T. F. Perception of environment. *Commission on College Geography Resource Paper No. 5.* Washington, D.C.: Association of American Geographers, 1969.

Stea, D. , & Downs, R. M. From the outside looking in at the inside looking out. *Environment and Behavior*, 1970, *1*, 3–12.

PART IV
SYNTHESIS

CHAPTER 10

Implications for the Field of Environment and Behavior

A fundamental implication of an explicit consideration of the perspective underlying a field of inquiry is that such an analysis engenders a fresh commitment to the particular character of that area's development. For the perspective behind a scientific enterprise will influence the type of investigative questions to be posed, the kinds of data to be sought, and the nature of the research answers that will be deemed acceptable. Ittelson, Franck, and O'Hanlon (1976) have eloquently articulated the relevance of this concern to the study of environment and behavior:

> So perhaps the principal methodological concern in our studies of environmental experience has been to become self-consciously aware of our preconceptions and of the influence that they will have on the outcome of any study. . . . Few other areas of study are so susceptible to the influence of the presuppositions of the investigator. If we uncritically assume on the basis of our personal and cultural history that we know the nature of the environment, then we will have inevitably written the answer into the way we ask the question (pp. 191–192).

It thus becomes imperative that we turn our attention now to a consideration of some ways in which the dynamic perspective we have discussed might influence the manner in which we conduct the study of environment and behavior. We will find that the dynamic perspective bears important implications for theory, research, and application in this field of study. For example, the dynamic perspective will influence theoretical development in environmental psychology that reflects and mirrors the dramatically active role of the person in confronting environmental challenges. In addition, the dynamic perspective will encourage the development of research strategies that are sufficiently flexible and varied to demonstrate a congruent relationship with the variety, complexity, and subtlety of human behavior in environmental contexts. Finally, in applying knowledge from environmental psychology to the solution of pressing social concerns, the dynamic perspective will foster an attitude on the part of the investigator that supports and enhances the active role of the individual in the environment–behavior picture.

This final chapter is divided into two major parts. The first part of the chapter begins with a summary of the dynamic processes of environmental coping, social accommodation, and environmental schematization. This is followed by the derivation of four postulates that integrate and synthesize the implications of our earlier discussion of the dynamic perspective for the investigative stance of the environmental psychologist. The second part of the chapter then pursues and discusses the significance of each of the derived postulates for the conduct of the study of environment and behavior in the spheres of theoretical development, research enterprise, and the practical application of scientific knowledge.

SUMMING UP WHERE WE HAVE BEEN

Coping with Environmental Challenges

In Part I, we examined the compelling drama in which environmental users actively engage in a diversity of positive coping strategies in dealing with environmental challenges. We saw how residents of a socially stagnating high-rise housing project managed to usurp any accessible open space to reinforce existing social needs. Children claimed an amphitheater for ball playing and adults congregated on city stoops to chat with neighbors, while nearby, functionally less relevant park spaces sat vacant. In a dissatisfying university megadorm, student residents evolved social coping strategies appropriate to counteracting the deleterious environmental effects. In response to the sense of social fragmentation engendered by the dormitory, residents developed spatially proximate and readily accessible friendship networks. Psychiatric staff in a large municipal hospital, after initially showing resistance to a large-scale ward remodeling, managed to cope effectively with the outsider-induced changes. Through a process of "personalization," the staff evolved a sense of personal responsibility, involvement, and control in the environmental change process.

Each of these examples reflected some of the ways in which people have learned to cope with the social isolation and deper-sonalization characteristic of so many contemporary environmental settings. In environmental coping, we observed individuals evolve a diversity of adaptive strategies that were able to convert potentially dehumanizing environments into socially positive and effective human contexts. Here, the human drama inherent in the dynamic perspective was most evident; environmental coping depicted human energy prevailing over environmental restraint.

Environmental coping evidenced especially clearly the active and human-initiated character of the dynamic perspective. In it we saw a dramatically high level of personal resourcefulness, determin-ation, and creativity. Thus, environmental coping reflected a process of *assimilation*, whereby environmental users adaptively wove the surrounding physical context into the fabric of their social life. An additional characteristic of environmental coping was the quality of its being tailored to individual needs, experiences, and skills. Different people evolved unique tactics in dealing with environmental demands that were congruent with personal abilities and personal styles of action. For example, we observed how environmental coping in a range of different environmental contexts varied in style as a function of personal characteristics such as age, social competence, and social status.

Subtle Accommodations to Environmental Constraint

Part II described the compelling process through which environmental users relinquished some degree of the intimacy of their social life in environmental settings where the adverse human consequences could not be wholly erased. We observed how in a poorly designed psychiatric setting, not only was the overall level of social contact reduced, but the very quality of interpersonal participation was subtly affected. When patients did interact socially in the poorly designed hospital environment, the nature of their contact was more distant, emotionally colder, and less intimate than in the well-designed social setting. In a university counseling setting, where poorly designed space allowed an invasion of the counselee's privacy, we saw that counselees were as verbally responsive as in more private circumstances; however, their conversation was less personally "immediate." With reduced privacy, respondents reverted to discussing the experiences of people in general or third parties rather than personal experiences of their own. In examining the notoriously low level of altruistic behavior associated with urban life, we found that the city's interpersonal distance was not, as has typically been assumed, a simple function of insensitivity on the part of the urban dweller. In fact, the reduced altruism of the city reflected a measured accommodation to the realities of the urban environment based on a careful weighing of personal risk relative to interpersonal need in the light of specific environmental circumstances.

Each of these episodes reflected the manner in which individuals restrict their interpersonal openness and sensitivity to accommodate the realistic constraints of environmental contexts that are so poorly designed relative to social need that even the most resourceful coping cannot wholly reverse their adverse human costs. Especially interesting was a realization that even in succumbing to environmental restraint, the inherently dynamic character of human action toward the environment remained apparent. For the process of yielding to the pressures of unavoidable environmental circumstances emerged as characterized by a high degree of complexity, subtlety, and even creativity.

A particularly compelling aspect of social accommodation was the observation that, although the process might appear intuitively to be quite simple, it is characteristically quite complex. We saw how this complexity might be evidenced at either the stage of weighing the antecedent conditions to accommodation or the point of determining the mode of the accommodating response. Social accommodation, in addition, demonstrated a high degree of unpredictability, tending to evolve in a subtle manner and at levels of social process where it was unanticipated. For example, social accommodation appeared often to unfold at less evident, more covert levels of experience, while failing to develop at more immediately evident planes of action. In each case, the behavioral outcomes reflected carefully achieved balances between social activity and environmental constraint.

Finally, we observed that social accommodation tended characteristically to unfold outside of human awareness. Even after demonstrating complex and subtle accommodations, environmental users themselves were often unaware that the process had occurred. Fascinatingly, the process of accommodating to environmental realities appeared to be so efficiently learned that without forethought or conscious decision the intimacy, warmth, and depth of people's interpersonal contact was subtly adjusted to accommodate environmental demands.

We have emphasized, thus far, the exciting and psychologically rich aspects of the social accommodation process. There is, however, another, more negative side to social accommodation. Precisely because social accommodation tends to evolve outside of conscious awareness, it may often involve hidden *long-term costs*. That is, environmental users may gradually attenuate the psychological closeness of their interpersonal contacts in such a way that initially minor accommodations accumulate over an extended period of time to represent a serious diminution in the quality of social life. Altman (1975), in referring to the work of Dubos (1965), notes similarly that the central question is not *whether* human beings can adjust to dire environmental conditions but rather what are the psychic and physical *costs* over the long run of such accommodations.

Uniquely Personal Environmental Schemata

In Part III, we investigated the manner in which environmental users evolved highly personalized and idiosyncratic schemata of the physical environment. We saw, for example, dramatic differences in the ways in which males and females schematize the environment, with women tending to view the environment in relatively more personal and more social terms than men. In addition, we discovered that even the physical maps that people draw of the environment betray a complex and active human involvement. We found that what at first appeared as accidental distortions in cognitive mapping were, in fact, subtle reconstructions of the physical environment in accord with corresponding variations in personal patterns of activity in the environment.

Environmental schematization represented a process whereby environmental users shaped, reconstructed, and organized the physical environment into a meaningful and personalized pattern. Through environmental schematization the individual was able to impose on the physical setting an array of personal feelings and attitudes. Thus, we came to realize that the very definition of the physical environment involved a complex human process, with the apparently simple act of environmental perception emerging as one of active management and personal creativity. We found, in fact, that a full appreciation of environment–behavior relationships needs to be founded on an adequate comprehension of how the environment is viewed by the particular observer. For to a considerable degree, environmental perception emerged as a personal and idiosyncratic process with different people experiencing uniquely different environments that varied as a function of personal experience.

Derived Postulates

What implications does the dynamic perspective hold for the conduct of inquiry in the field of environment and behavior? To answer this question we must shift the focus of our inquiry from the behavior of the environmental user to that of the environmental scientist. In fact, our discussion of the dynamic perspective may be synthesized in the form of four postulates that derive directly from our previous analysis, and bear immediately on the nature of the investigative stance of the environmental scientist. In effect, the four postulates will represent orientations on the part of the environmental scientist to particular aspects of the manner in which environmental phenomena will be approached. The postulates may thus be viewed as "metaprinciples" in environmental psychology. That is, they describe the character of the scientific enterprise itself, rather than the nature of the investigated subject matter.

At a general level, the four postulates reflect an overarching sensitivity on the part of the environmental psychologist to the unique role of the person in the environment–behavior equation. Although all of the postulates are relevant to all three of the dynamic processes we have considered, we will see that each of the first three postulates bears a particularly immediate relationship to one of the dynamic processes. For example, postulate one pertains to the *active* stance of the individual toward the environment and relates most directly to the process of environmental coping. Postulate two reflects the rich *complexity* of environmental behavior and is most closely related to the social accommodation process. The *subjective* dimension in environmental action is captured in postulate three, which relates most immediately to environmental schematization. Postulate four, which pertains to the *uniquely* personal character of behavior in environmental contexts, bears equal relevance to all three dynamic processes.

Postulate One. The environmental psychologist will adopt a viewpoint that reflects the active, creative, and problem-solving role of the individual in initiating environment-directed behavior.

Postulate Two. The environmental psychologist will assume

an analytical posture that is congruent with the rich complexity, diversity, and subtlety of environmental behavior.

  Postulate Three. The environmental psychologist will adopt an investigative attitude that mirrors the vantage point of the environmental user, reflecting the purposive, meaningful, and goal-directed character of human behavior toward the environment.

  Postulate Four. The environmental psychologist will assume a conceptual position that reflects the transactional influence of both personal uniqueness and environmental diversity in shaping human activity in environmental contexts.

  Let us turn now to a consideration of the potential impact of these postulates on the conduct of inquiry in the field of environment and behavior in three spheres of endeavor — theory, research, and application. In each of these realms of professional activity, we will pursue in turn the implications of each of the four derived postulates. In effect, we will use the analytical focus provided by the postulates as intellectual anchoring points around which to organize and reflect on some exciting developments in environmental psychology that are particularly congruent with the thrust of the perspective discussed here. It is hoped that such an integrative analysis will both legitimize and enhance the potentially vital role of the dynamic perspective in the evolving development of our field of study. It is anticipated, in addition, that this discussion will suggest a number of avenues of inquiry on the part of readers who feel inclined to pursue further a consideration of environment and behavior from a dynamic perspective.

IMPLICATIONS FOR THE STUDY OF ENVIRONMENT AND BEHAVIOR

Theoretical Development

  Agentic Viewpoint. A potentially fruitful conceptual framework for considering the active, agentic posture of people in the environmental context is offered in Stokols's (in press) recent discussion of "human-environment optimization." Human-environment optimization refers to the ways in which individuals and groups attempt to achieve optimal environments, that is, environments that maximize the fulfilling of their goals and needs. Stokols, in integrating and extending earlier work by Altman (1976) and Miller, Galanter, and Pribram (1960), postulates that there are three essential modes of human interaction with the environment — orientation, operation, and evaluation. He notes that these processes reflect the active stance of people in perceiving, shaping, and evaluating their environmental surroundings in the light of personal needs. While Stokols points out that human-environment optimization is not in itself a *theory* of human-environment transactions, he suggests that the concept provides a useful framework for integrating a wide diversity of past research in environmental psychology around the themes of orientation, operation, and evaluation.

Stokols notes, for example, that the manner in which people orient toward the environment is emphasized in research on environmental perception (cf. Ittelson, 1973), cognitive mapping (cf. Downs & Stea, 1973; Lynch. 1960), and the assessment of social climate (cf. Moos, 1973; Insel & Moos, 1974). The ways in which people operate on and are affected by the environment is demonstrated in research on spatial behavior (cf. Altman, 1975; Hall, 1966; Sommer, 1969; Stokols, 1976) and the effects of environmental stressors (Glass & Singer, 1972; Sherrod, 1974; Stokols, 1972). Finally, Stokols suggests that the manner in which people evaluate the environment is reflected in research on environmental assessment and preference (cf. Craik, 1971, 1976) and social impact assessment (cf. Catalano, Simmons, & Stokols, 1975; Wolf, 1974, 1975).

Multilevel Analysis. Altman and Taylor (1973) offer a theoretical position that is especially congruent with the multilevel complexity of environmental behavior. They propose the notion of "social penetration" as an organizing conceptual framework for understanding how social relationships progress through the stages of stranger, casual acquaintance, close friend, and beyond. Most importantly, they contend that the social penetration process should be viewed as a system, which involves the simultaneous operation of behavior across a number of different levels of response, including verbal behavior, nonverbal behavior, and environmentally oriented behavior. In discussing social penetration, Altman and Taylor emphasize that our understanding of the development of interpersonal relationships necessitates an analysis of the whole person, in contrast to isolated segments of behavior. They note that different levels of social behavior operate in "unison," sometimes complementing one another and sometimes substituting for one another sequentially.

Altman (1975), in analyzing the phenomenon of privacy, provides a compelling example of how social relationships unfold simultaneously on multiple levels of experience. He notes that people attempt to achieve desired levels of privacy by employing verbal, nonverbal, and environmental behaviors "as an integrated system in much the same way as the instruments and sections of a symphony orchestra yield an integrated result" (p. 32). For example, people maintain a desired degree of privacy through verbal messages, such as: "keep out," "I need to be left alone," "I have a secret I want to share with you." In addition, nonverbal behavior may be used to achieve privacy. Altman reports a field study (Patterson, Mullens, & Romano, 1971) involving an invasion of students' personal space in a library, which showed that with increased intrusion, subjects responded by glaring, leaning or orienting away, and using their arms to block themselves off from the intruder. Finally, people actively use the physical environment in seeking a desired level of privacy, altering, for example, their interpersonal distance or wearing clothing and personal adornment that convey a desired sense of status and distance.

Phenomenological Attitude. Koffka's (1935) concept of the "behavioral environment" represented the first psychological discussion of the environment as viewed or experienced phenomenologically, in contrast to the objective or geographic environment. Later, Lewin (1936) in his field theoretical view of the "psychological environment" more fully developed a theory of psychological reality. Lewin emphasized that in order to fully appreciate human behavior we must account adequately for the environment as it is perceived by the individual.

> Even when from the standpoint of the physicist, the environment is identical or nearly identical for a child and for an adult, the psychological situation can be fundamentally different ... the situation must be represented in the way in which it is real for the individual in question, that is, as it affects him (Lewin, 1936, pp. 24–25).

There is a particular need in environmental psychology for research addressed toward the environment as it is uniquely experienced and appreciated from the vantage point of particular environmental users. The investigations in the area of cognitive mapping discussed in Chapter 9 represent one important body of environmental research in this area.

An additional notable body of investigation in the field of environment and behavior which reflects a phenomenological orientation is research that has been concerned with the perceived *psychosocial climate* in a range of different environmental settings. For example, Moos (1973) and his associates at Stanford's Social Ecology Laboratory have developed perceived climate scales appropriate to the measurement of the general norms, value orientation, and psychosocial characteristics of a wide range of settings, including psychiatric wards, community-oriented treatment programs, correctional institutions, university residences, work environments, and family settings. Moos has conceptualized three basic categories of dimensions that characterize the psychosocial climate in such settings. *Relationship* dimensions assess perceived social involvement, support, and help in the environment. Individuals' perceptions of the opportunity in the setting for self-enhancement and the development of self-esteem is measured by *personal development* dimensions. Finally, system *maintenance and change* dimensions reflect the perceived social psychological impact of the formal organizational structure.

It should be emphasized that we are not proposing an exclusively phenomenological perspective as appropriate for environmental psychology. Our concern is that the objectivist view of the environment be complemented by a phenomenological orientation. In effect, both perspectives are essential, each yielding unique data in the total environmental framework. As Pervin

(1968) has noted, the history of psychology has been characterized by exaggerated and fruitless extremes of these two positions — behaviorism versus introspectionism; stimulus-response theory versus psychoanalysis; role theory versus need theory. Ittelson *et al.* (1976) propose a unifying conceptual framework that eschews the traditional proclivity of the environmental scientist to artificially dichotomize person from environment and experience from action. They note:

> Environmental experience is the continuing product of an active endeavour by the individual to create for himself a situation within which he can optimally function and achieve his own particular pattern of satisfaction. We believe it is particularly important for us as scientists not to accept any particular mode of environmental experience as representing a true [or complete] picture of the environment (p. 206).

Transactional Position. Closely related to the historical tendency for psychologists to polarize on the objectivist–subjectivist controversy has been the penchant for extreme psychological camps to evolve around the issue of how best to predict human behavior. Ekehammar (1974) offers a useful historical perspective on this question. He refers to *personologism* as the position advocating stable, intraorganismic "traits" as the primary determinants of human behavior. He adds that *situationism* presents the antithesis of personologism, emphasizing environmental variables as dominant in shaping behavioral variation. Finally, Ekehammar describes *interactionism* as the synthesis of the two extreme views, postulating that the essential source of variance in human behavior is a function of the interaction of both personal and environmental forces. Historically, the interactionist position in psychology was most fully discussed in the writings of Lewin (1935) and Murray (1938).

Endler and Magnusson (1976) emphasize a fundamental characteristic of interactionism that bears particular relevance to our discussion of the dynamic perspective. "*Reciprocal causation* means that not only do events affect the behavior of organisms but the organism is also an active agent in influencing environmental events" (p. 969). They note that much interactionist research has tended to cast the person in a passive role at the prey of environmental forces. They stress the need for models reflecting multidirectional causality, underscoring Pervin's (1968) suggestion that the term *transaction* be employed in referring to the process of reciprocal causation. Thus our use of the term *transactional* is intended to reflect the dynamic, two-way interaction between the person and the environment. Of course, this view does not imply that in every transaction personal and situational factors are of equal importance. In fact, the question of how much behavioral variance in a particular situation is a function of personal and environmental variables, respectively, is an empirical one, and has been the focus of an important body of environmental research beginning in the early 1960s.

This empirically based interactionist research has involved a number of measurement strategies, including field observational studies (Raush, Dittmann, & Taylor, 1959a, 1959b; Raush, Farbman & Llewellyn, 1960), a paper-and-pencil index of anxiousness across a range of situations (Endler & Hunt, 1966, 1968, 1969), and analyses of both self-ratings and observational data in psychiatric ward settings (Moos, 1968, 1969, 1970). The conclusions of all of this research have been remarkably similar; behavioral prediction needs to be viewed as a combination of a number of different sources of variance, including variance due to both the person and the situation and, most significantly, to the person × situation interaction. After 30 years of often fruitless controversy, psychologists have rediscovered the essential wisdom of Lewin's (1936) basic dictum, $B = f(P,E)$, that is, behavior is a function of both the person and the environment.

Research Strategy

Unchaining the Research Subject. A commitment to recognizing the active nature of environmental behavior is especially relevant to the manner in which environmental research is conducted. For an unfortunate consequence of applying conventional psychological research strategies in studying environment and behavior has been a tendency for the research subject to emerge as a passive pawn in the play of overwhelming environmental forces. In fact, our experimental hypotheses may often be confirmed only because we have so carefully arranged the experimental situation that all alternative response options are eliminated. Mahler (1974) has referred to this phenomenon in psychological research as the bull in the Royal Worcester china shop. With the hypothesis that bulls are characterized by a desire to break Royal Worcester china, we stock the shop exclusively with that item, turn the bulls loose, and watch the ensuing destruction. Our hypothesis is duly confirmed — especially if our control group is mice" (p. 2).

Simply moving environmental research from the laboratory to the field is insufficient. The *manner* in which field-based research is conducted is essential to a full appreciation of the active role of the person in the environment–behavior chain. Proshansky (1976) notes that too often pyschological field research has simply shifted the paradigm of the laboratory to the field setting. He adds that what is required are new investigative methods and techniques able to reflect holistically the role of the individual in an inter-actional stance toward a patterned environmental context. Such research strategies will need to be sufficiently open-ended at the response end to permit the subject a wide range of alternative response options, including positive coping responses and problem-solving behaviors. Bronfenbrenner (1976) notes that ecologically relevant field research will require investigative strategies that preserve the ecological integrity of the settings studied, avoiding the introduction of artificially extraneous elements that distort the holistic meaning of the setting to participants.

Gump and Kounin (1960), in fact, report a case of a field research project (Gump & Sutton-Smith, 1955) where conditions artificially arranged by the investigators led to statistically significant, though highly contrived, experimental findings. The investigators were interested in the reactions of poorly skilled players in difficult game roles. They studied the phenomenon by assigning slow runners to the *it* position in a game of tag, and confirmed their hypothesis that the degree of power permitted to the *it* position affected both the poorly skilled players' success and the amount of scapegoating they encountered. Later, Gump and

Kounin observed children in a range of different naturalistic game settings. They observed that:

> (a) Poorly skilled boys do not often get involved in games they cannot manage; (b) if they do get involved, they often manage to avoid difficult roles by not trying to win such a position or by quitting if they cannot avoid it; and (c) if they occupy the role and are having trouble, the game often gets so boring to opponents that these opponents let themselves be caught in order to put the game back on a more zestful level (p. 148).

Multiple Operationism. The blind Liza in Lawrence Durrell's *Clea*, after resting her head on her departed brother's pillow, comments: "I wanted to try and take his imprint from the pillow. . . . One must try everything to recover memory. It has so many hidingplaces" (p. 220). Similarly, the environmental researcher needs to develop a sensitivity to the multiple levels through which environmental behavior expresses itself — verbal expressions, nonverbal bodily responses and gestures, and physical traces in the environment. In fact, adequate measurement in environmental psychology will necessitate a number of "converging measures," where different measurement techniques complement one another in capturing the diverse facets of environmental behavior. Webb, Campbell, Schwartz, and Sechrest (1966) arrive at a similar conclusion in addressing this issue in terms of the inherent weaknesses in any simple measurement strategy.

> Today, some 90 percent of social science research is based upon interviews and questionnaires. We lament this overdependence upon a single, fallible method. . . . *But the principle objection is that they are used alone.* No research method is without bias . . . the issue is not choosing among individual methods. Rather it is the necessity for a multiple operationism, a collection of methods combined to avoid sharing the same weaknesses (pp. 1–2).

Research strategies based on a multiple operationism are especially appropriate to the evaluation of the potential hidden costs that may be a consequence of environmental change. For, oftentimes, it may be that effective, immediate adjustments to environmental change are vitiated by long-term costs across alternative levels of response. For example, Ittelson, Rivlin, and

Proshansky (1970) report a field study involving the environmental remodeling of an underused solarium in a municipal psychiatric hospital. An initial evaluation corroborated change expectations, indicating that active social behavior had significantly increased in the solarium during the postremodeling period. However, further measurement in other areas of the ward indicated that, simultaneous with the increase in social behaviors in the solarium, there had been a dramatic increase in passive-isolated behavior at the opposite end of the ward! In addition, Glass and Singer (1972) discuss a study of the psychological effects of exposure to random and unpredictable high-intensity noise. While immediate, successful adaptation occurred during the noise period itself, psychological consequences appeared later in poor performance in other areas *after* the cessation of noise!

   User Input. A phenomenological orientation in environmental psychology encourages the development of research strategies appropriate to assessing user reactions and input in the environmental design process. The role of the environmental researcher in this realm is complex. For while user input in the design process is a laudable goal, as Proshansky, Ittelson, and Rivlin (1970) have observed, environmental users are often unaware of the pervasive influence of the surrounding environmental context. Thus, an initial agenda of the researcher will involve facilitating an environmental sensitivity on the part of users commensurate with their potential role in the planning process. In fact, Sommer (1972) has proposed that environmental psychologists might conduct environmental workshops oriented toward educating users to the ways in which they might shape their environmental settings. Sommer reports some fascinating results from a workshop where hospital staff were induced to play the role of patients as a means of empathizing with patients' perspectives of the hospital environment:

> As turn-on devices we used such prosthetic aids as crutches, wheelchairs, and gurneys. These produced some interesting perceptual experiences which were shared with the group at large. Distances seemed three times as long on crutches as they had previously. It took a very long time to go down the hallway in a wheel-

chair; when one person wheeled another, the speed of passage was very important. Wheeling a person at ordinary walking speed seemed much too fast; the person in the chair felt as if he were a bowling ball going down the alley. Tall men were particularly bothered by being looked down on as they sat in a wheelchair (p. 44).

Once users have acquired a full sensitivity to environmental influences, a further, and somewhat innovative, implication of the dynamic perspective in research underscores the potentially constructive role of users in designing environmental research. For example, users might be employed as consultants in selecting the appropriate dimensions for measurement in particular environmental settings. Users might also be engaged in determining the wording and phrasing of self-report items most appropriate for the population investigated. One wonders how often the failure to achieve significant results in environmental research or, conversely, the attaining of atypical and confusing significant effects may not simply reflect an essential irrelevance of the measurement dimensions to the user group. Finally, Wilson and Donnerstein (1976), in reflecting on potential ethical problems associated with nonreactive field research methods, propose as one solution to the ethical dilemma giving representatives from the subject population a major voice in determining the research strategy.

Interactional Research. A pressing initial agenda for environmental research in an interactional framework will be the development of more sophisticated investigative tools in two essential areas. First, the historical neglect of the physical environment as a sphere for psychological research, particularly when contrasted with the considerable energy devoted to the measurement of individual differences, has resulted in a marked imbalance in our relative ability to precisely measure person and environment. Thus, an immediate task essential to interactionist research is the generation of a comparable conceptual clarity and psychometric precision on the environmental side of the equation. Moos (1973) suggests an initial conceptualization of the environment along six basic sets of characteristics: ecology (architecture and geography), behavior settings, organizational structure, population characteristics, psychosocial climate, and functional analyses.

Interactional research will necessitate, in addition, a methodological sophistication commensurate with tne analytical complexity of multivariate designs, reciprocal causality, and higher-order interactions. Psychologists will need to stray outside of the methodological security of the analysis of variance and to take advantage of some statistical techniques already available for dealing with complex data bases. Helmreich (1975) suggests the utility of path analysis, which uses multiple regression techniques to estimate the parameters of an explicit causal model, and auto- and cross-lagged correlations, which assess the covariation of variables over time. Helmreich encourages more sophisticated use by psychologists of tools such as the *Statistical Package for the Social Sciences* (Nie, Hull, Jenkins, Steinbrenner, & Bent, 1975), which offers a capability to handle, edit, and transform as many as 1,000 variables with programs such as analysis of variance, factor analysis, multiple regression, and path analysis. In addition, Hiese (1975) presents a highly readable introduction to the logic and statistical methodology appropriate to the analysis of complex casual relationships.

APPLICATION: TOWARD A SOCIALLY RELEVANT ENVIRONMENTAL PSYCHOLOGY

One of the most compelling challenges facing behavioral science today is the need to determine the character of our stance toward society. In fact, a recent study sponsored by the National Academy of Sciences and the Social Science Research Council (1969) has underscored the need for a major effort on the part of the behavioral sciences oriented toward the application of scientific knowledge to the solution of social problems. The dynamic postulates we have discussed in this chapter bear some important implications relevant to the stance of the environmental psychologist toward society. Here, the challenge is less one of science than of confronting the underlying social values, commitment, and responsibility that guide the scientific process as a human enterprise.

The dynamic perspective's emphasis, for example, on the positive, agentic character of environmental behavior suggests the need for an applied psychology to enhance rather than tarnish society's image of the person. Regretably, as Sanford (1970) has cautioned, the manner in which psychologists have approached social issues has too often resulted in our disseminating an image of the person as fragmented and externalized. The dynamic perspective, in contrast, fosters a view of the person as competent, responsible, and resourceful. Of course, this viewpoint needs to be balanced by a realistic appraisal of environmental blocks to achievement. As Ryan (1971) and Caplan and Nelson (1973) have observed, the tendency of well-meaning psychologists to focus exclusively on person-centered variables has too often obscured an awareness of contemporary institutional obstacles to the achievement of an acceptable quality of life for disenfranchised groups.

The focus of the dynamic perspective on the multilevel complexity of human action toward the environment highlights the need that the societal application of psychological knowledge constitute an interdisciplinary effort. Proshansky (1972) contends that psychology must relinquish its discipline purity and recognize that discipline boundaries are founded on traditional academic structures rather than the character of social problems. Proshansky goes on, however, to emphasize that graduate education be rooted in a particular discipline, and eschews a "cafeteria" approach to interdisciplinary training:

> . . . the purpose of the interdisciplinary curriculum focus for a given area of specialization is to provide the psychology student with selected concepts, methods, and approaches of other disciplines so as to extend and deepen his understanding of his own substantive problem area in psychology. The essential objective is not to make him a generalist, but to prevent him from developing into the narrow kind of specialist (p. 211).

Our discussion of the environmental user's perspective encourages, in addition, an awareness on the part of the psychologist of social concern at a broader level. Initially, such social sensitivity will necessitate a change in our prevailing professional reward structure in the social sciences to accord research productivity of a policy-oriented nature a degree of scientific status consonant with that granted basic research (Proshansky, 1972; Willems, 1971). Implicit in this is a need to recognize that social policy problems often require innovative investigative strategies and tactics not fashionable in academic social science. In addition, social scientists will have to achieve a balance between the scientific ideal of research that is self-initiated and free of outside restraint, and the reality that applied research needs to be open to community values, needs, and input.

Our consideration of a transactional position, integrating the influences of both person and environment, intimates a broader need for psychological theories that are both problem-centered and "grounded" in real life experience. A socially relevant psychology will need to advance theory that has been tested and refined in the context of the practical affairs of life. Kurt Lewin once commented, "I am persuaded that if the scientist proceeds correctly, a close link with practice can be a blessing for the development of theory (Marrow, 1969, p. 172). Proshansky (1972) suggests an innovative working relationship between new problem-oriented training programs in psychology and their surrounding community, which is reminiscent of Lewin's (1947) notion of action research:

> I am recommending something more sweeping: namely, that we open our own programs to the community in the sense that we evolve cooperative relationships with them, directed toward providing them with the expertise of an interdisciplinary faculty, and they in turn providing us with the opportunities to involve our students in community-based curricular, administrative, and research experiences on a *continuing* basis (p. 211).

Psychology celebrates its one hundredth birthday as a science in 1979. The century since the inception of Wundt's psychological laboratory in Leipzig has marked a period of outstanding success for psychology in the academic and scientific communities. Unfortunately, however, as Proshansky (1972) has cautioned, in its stance toward society, psychology has too often fallen short of its promises. For the high expectations that psychological expertise would prove applicable to the resolution of the major problems of society have not been achieved. As psychology advances into its second century, the need to integrate high scientific merit with social relevance will present a foremost challenge. These are exciting times to be involved in environmental psychology, for we have innovative theories to evolve, new field methods to devise, and promises to keep.

REFERENCES

Altman, I. *The environmental and social behavior: Privacy, personal space, territory and crowding.* Monterey, California: Brooks / Cole, 1975.

Altman, I. Environmental psychology and social psychology. *Personality and Social Psychology Bulletin,* 1976, *2,* 96–113.

Altman, I., & Taylor, D. A. *Social penetration: The development of interpersonal relationships.* New York: Holt, Rinehart & Winston, 1973.

Bronfenbrenner, U. The experimental ecology of education. *Educational Researcher,* 1976, *5,* 5–15.

Caplan, N., & Nelson, S. C. On being useful: The nature and consequences of psychological research on social problems. *American Psychologist,* 1973, *28,* 199–211.

Catalano, R., Simmons, S., & Stokols, D. Adding social science knowledge to environmental decision making. *Natural Resources Lawyer,* 1975, *8,* 41–59.

Craik, K. The assessment of places. In P. McReynolds (Ed.), *Advances in psychological assessment.* Palo Alto: Science and Behavior Books, 1971.

Craik, K. The personality research paradigm in environmental psychology. In S. Wapner, S. B. Cohen, & B. Kaplan (Eds.), *Experiencing the environment.* New York: Plenum, 1976.

Downs, R., & Stea, D. *Image and environment: Cognitive mapping and spatial behavior.* Chicago: Aldine, 1973.

Dubos, R. *Man adapting.* New Haven: Yale University Press, 1965.

Durrell, L. *Clea.* New York: Dutton, 1961.

Ekehammar, B. Interactionism in personality from a historical perspective. *Psychological Bulletin,* 1974, *81,* 1026–1048.

Endler, N. S., & Hunt, J. McV. Sources of behavioral variance as measured by the S-R inventory of anxiousness. *Psychological Bulletin,* 1966, *65,* 336–346.

Endler, N. S., & Hunt, J. Mc.V. S-R inventories of hostility and comparisons of the proportions of variance from persons, responses and situations for hostility and anxiousness. *Journal of Personality and Social Psychology,* 1968, *9,* 114–123.

Endler, N. S., & Hunt, J. McV. Generalizability of contributions from sources of variance in the S-R inventories of anxiousness. *Journal of Personality,* 1969, *37,* 1–24.

Endler, N. S., & Magnusson, D. Toward an interactional psychology of personality. *Psychological Bulletin*, 1976, *83*, 956–974.

Glass, D., & Singer, J. *Urban stress*. New York: Academic Press, 1972.

Gump, P. V., & Kounin, J. S. Issues raised by ecological and "classical" research efforts. *Merrill-Palmer Quarterly*, 1960, *6*, 145–152.

Gump, P. V., & Sutton-Smith, B. The "it" role in children's games. *The Group*, 1955, *17*, 3–8.

Hall, E. *The hidden dimension*. New York: Doubleday, 1966.

Helmreich, R. Applied social psychology: The unfulfilled promise. *Personality and Social Psychology Bulletin*, 1975, *1* (4), 548–560.

Heise, D. R. *Causal analysis*. New York: Wiley, 1975.

Insel, P., & Moos, R. Psychological environments: Expanding the scope of human ecology. *American Psychologist*, 1974, *29*, 179–188.

Ittelson, W. *Environment and cognition*. New York: Seminar Press, 1973.

Ittelson, W. H., Franck, K. A., & O'Hanlon, T. J. The nature of environmental experience. In S. Wapner, S. B. Cohen, & B. Kaplan Eds., *Experiencing the environment*. New York: Plenum, 1976.

Ittelson, W. H., Rivlin, L. G., & Proshansky, H. M. The use of behavioral maps in environmental psychology. In H. M. Proshansky, W. H. Ittelson, & L. G. Rivlin (Eds.), *Environmental psychology: Man and his physical setting*. New York: Holt, Rinehart & Winston, 1970.

Koffka, K. *Principles of Gestalt psychology*. New York: Harcourt, Brace, & World, 1935.

Lewin, K. *A dynamic theory of personality: Selected papers*. New York: McGraw-Hill, 1935.

Lewin, K. *Principles of topological psychology*. New York: McGraw-Hill, 1936.

Lewin, K. Group decision and social change. In T. M. Newcomb & E. L. Hartley (Eds.), *Reading in social psychology*. New York: Holt, Rinehart & Winston, 1947.

Lynch, K. *The image of the city*. Cambridge, Massachusetts: M.I.T. Press, 1960.

Mahler, B. Editorial. *Journal of Consulting and Clinical Psychology*, 1974, *42*, 1–3.

Marrow, A. J. *The practical theorist: The life and work of Kurt Lewin*. New York: Basic Books, 1969.

Miller, G., Galanter, E., and Pribram, K. *Plans and the structure of behavior*. New York: Holt, Rinehart & Winston, 1960.

Moos, R. H. Situational analysis of a therapeutic community milieu. *Journal of Abnormal Psychology*, 1968, *73*, 49–61.

Moos, R. H. Sources of variance in responses to questionnaires and in behavior. *Journal of Abnormal Psychology*, 1969, *74*, 405–412.

Moos, R. H. Differential effects of psychiatric ward settings on patient change. *Journal of Nervous and Mental Disease*, 1970, *5*, 316–321.

Moos, R. H. Conceptualizations of human environments. *American Psychologist*, 1973, *28*, 652–665.

Moos, R. H. Evaluating and changing community settings. *American Journal of Community Psychology*, 1976, *4*, 313–326.

Murray, H. A. *Explorations in personality*. New York: Oxford University Press, 1938.

National Academy of Sciences and Social Science Research Council. *The behavioral and social sciences: Outlook and needs*. Englewood Cliffs, New Jersey: Prentice-Hall, 1969.

Nie, N. H., Hull, C. H., Jenkins, J. G., Steinbrenner, K., & Bent, D. H. *SPSS: Statistical package for the social sciences*. New York: McGraw-Hill, 1975.

Patterson, M L., Mullens, S., & Romano, J. Compensatory reactions to spatial intrusion. *Sociometry*, 1971, *34*, 114–121.

Pervin, L. A. Performance and satisfaction as a function of individual-environment fit. *Psychological Bulletin*, 1968, *69*, 56–68.

Proshansky, H. M. For what are we training our graduate students? *American Psychologist*, 1972, *27*, 205–212.

Proshansky, H. M. Environmental psychology and the real world. *American Psychologist*, 1976, *31*, 303–310.

Proshansky, H. M., Ittelson, W. H., & Rivlin, L. G. The influence of the physical environment on behavior: Some basic assumptions. In H. M. Proshansky, W. H. Ittelson, & L. G. Rivlin (Eds.), *Environmental psychology: Man and his physical setting*. New York: Holt, Rinehart & Winston, 1970.

Raush, H. L., Dittmann, A. T., & Taylor, T. J. The interpersonal behavior of children in residential treatment. *Journal of Abnormal and Social Psychology*, 1959, *58*, 9–26. (a)

Raush, H. L., Dittmann, A. T., & Taylor, T. J. Person, setting and change in social interaction. *Human Relations*, 1959, *12*, 361–378. (b)

Raush, H. L., Farbman, I., & Llewellyn, L. G. Person, setting and change in social interaction: II: A normal-control study. *Human Relations*, 1960, *13*, 305–332.

Ryan, W. *Blaming the victim*. New York: Vintage Books, 1971.

Sanford, N. Whatever happened to action research? *Journal of Social Issues*, 1970, *26*, 3–23.

Sherrod, D. Crowding, perceived control and behavioral aftereffects. *Journal of Applied Social Psychology*, 1974, *4*, 171–186.

Sommer, R. *Personal space: The behavioral basis of design*. Englewood Cliffs, New Jersey: Prentice-Hall, 1969.

Sommer, R. *Design awareness*. New York: Holt, Rinehart & Winston, 1972.

Stokols, D. A social-psychological model of human crowding phenomena. *Journal of the American Institute of Planners*, 1972, *38*, 72–84.

Stokols, D. Social-unit analysis as a framework for research in environmental and social pyschology. *Personality and Social Psychology Bulletin*, in press.

Stokols, D. The experience of crowding in primary and secondary environments. *Environment and Behavior*, 1976, *8*, 49–86.

Webb, E. J., Campbell, D. T., Schwartz, R. D., & Sechrest, L. *Unobtrusive measures: Nonreactive research in the social sciences.* Chicago: Rand McNally, 1966.

Willems, W. *Social policy research and analysis: The experience in the federal social agencies.* New York: American Elsevier, 1971.

Wilson, D. W., & Donnerstein, E. Legal and ethical aspects of nonreactive social psychological research: An excursion into the public mind. *American Psychologist,* 1976, *31,* 765–773.

Wolf, C. Social impact assessment. In D. Carson (Ed.), *Man–environment interactions: Evaluation and applications* Vol. 2. Milwaukee: Environmental Design and Research Association, 1974.

Wolf, C. Editorial preface. *Environment and Behavior,* 1975, *7,* 259–263.

Author Index

Subject Index

166   137

Accommodation. *See* Social accommodation
Agentic approach, 168–169
Agentic mode, 134, 139
Allocentric milieu, 134, 139
Altruism, 77–79, 115, 119–122, 125, 164
Architecture and behavior, 3, 4, 6. *See also*
    Built environment; Design
Assimilation, 23, 163
Autocentric milieu, 134, 139

Behavior
    collective, 144–145, 147–148, 150–151,
       156–157
    microinterpersonal, 6–8
    personal, 144–147, 151–154, 156–157
Behavior mapping, 33–35
Behavioral environment, 133–134, 170
Behavioral science, challenges for, 178–181
Built environment, 5–9

Centrifugal distortion, 152–154
Change, impact of, 57, 50–70
Cognitive mapping, 7, 130–131, 143–157,
    166, 169
Communal mode, 134, 139
Competence
    environmental, 67–68
    social, 46–48, 51–54
Coping. *See* Environmental coping
Crowding, 2, 6, 8, 45
Counseling. *See* Setting, counseling
    (university)

Design, 3, 4, 11
    and hospitals, 57–58, 69, 95
    and university dormitories, 7, 46
    urban, 41–43
Dormitories. *See* Setting, university
    megadorm

Environment and behavior, theories of,
    168–173. *See also* Environmental
    psychology
Environmental coping, 10–12, 19–24, 75,
    110–111, 130, 162, 167
    features of, 22–24
    in high-rise public housing, 25–43
    in a psychiatric hospital, 57–70
    in a university megadorm, 45–55, 163
    in an urban setting, 162–163
Environmental perception, 169
Environmental psychology
    definition of, 9
    development of, 2, 5
    implications of, 161–162, 167–171,
       178–181
    postulates of, 167–68
    research strategies for, 6–10, 173–175,
       176–177
Environmental satisfaction, in a dormitory
    setting, 46–47, 49, 50–54
Environmental schematization
    features of, 130–132, 162, 167
    measures of, 136–137
    and sex-differences, 130–141